I Remember Judy, a love story

I Remember Judy, a love story

Verwayne Greenhoe

Fresh Ink Group
Guntersville

I Remember Judy, a love story

Copyright © 2024
by Verwayne Greenhoe
All rights reserved

Fresh Ink Group
An Imprint of:
The Fresh Ink Group, LLC
1021 Blount Avenue #931
Guntersville, AL 35976
Email: info@FreshInkGroup.com
FreshInkGroup.com

Edition 1.0 2024

Cover design by Stephen Geez / FIG
Book design by Amit Dey / FIG
Associate publisher Beem Weeks / FIG

Except as permitted under the U.S. Copyright Act of 1976 and except for brief quotations in critical reviews or articles, no portion of this book's content may be stored in any medium, transmitted in any form, used in whole or part, or sourced for derivative works such as videos, television, and motion pictures, without prior written permission from the publisher.

Cataloging-in-Publication Recommendations:
BIO026000 BIOGRAPHY & AUTOBIOGRAPHY / Memoirs
FAM030000 FAMILY & RELATIONSHIPS / Marriage & Long-Term Relationships
FAM014000 FAMILY & RELATIONSHIPS / Death, Grief, Bereavement

Library of Congress Control Number: 2024915073

ISBN-13: 978-1-964998-02-2 Softcover
ISBN-13: 978-1-964998-03-9 Hardcover
ISBN-13: 978-1-964998-04-6 Ebooks

Forward

This is the story of my life with Judy, a most beautiful woman who became my wife for over forty-some years. We raised two beautiful children and enjoyed a lifetime of memories. Sadly, toward the end, she couldn't remember them anymore.

Although I knew something was going wrong much earlier than that fateful day in January 2014, things got worse faster after that day. Judy had been an OB RN for forty-four years, and with no bravado talk, she was a darn good nurse.

She was always known for her calm and cool behavior during the worst obstetrical emergencies. The doctors who worked with her knew her instincts regarding a pending delivery were almost always on the mark.

It was such an emergency delivery the day everything went wrong. She was in a surgical room assisting with an emergency Cesarean Section, as she had done so many times before. The newborn was removed from the womb and was just seconds from having the baby handed to her when, according to those present, Judy stiffened up and fell over backward.

She was taken to the Emergency Room, and during her treatment, an MRI found what the radiologist termed 'significant white matter changes in the ventricles of her brain.' After a few hours, she was released from the ER and sent home. She was given an appointment with a neurologist in a nearby town.

The first thing we were told was that the specialist thought she had suffered a minor stroke but might also have Multiple Sclerosis or 'MS.' Later tests proved she was developing dementia and several other neurological disorders. To get those things out of the way, allow me to define each suspected disease process using Wikipedia. Don't worry; there won't be a test.

Let's start with MS. The initial attacks are often transient, mild, or show no symptoms at all and are self-limited. They frequently do not prompt a health care visit and sometimes are only identified in retrospect once the diagnosis has been made after further attacks.

The most common initial symptoms reported are changes in sensation in the arms, legs, or face, complete or partial vision loss, weakness, double vision, unsteadiness when walking, and balance problems. Many rare initial symptoms have been reported, such as aphasia or psychosis.

Aphasia is often called dysphasia, where a person may be unable to comprehend or unable to formulate language because of damage to specific brain regions. The disease is usually brought on by a stroke or head trauma. Fifteen percent of individuals have multiple symptoms when they first seek medical attention.

Psychosis is when the brain has difficulties determining what is real, and what is not. Frequent symptoms include delusions and hallucinations. Other symptoms may include incoherent speech and behavior that is inappropriate for a situation.

Multiple sclerosis can cause a variety of symptoms, including changes in sensation, muscle weakness, abnormal muscle spasms, or difficulty moving; difficulties with coordination and balance; problems in speech or swallowing; visual problems; fatigue and acute or chronic pain syndromes; bladder and bowel difficulties; cognitive impairment; or emotional symptomatology, mainly major depression.

After her situation got worse, further tests found that she also had a mixture of dementia, Alzheimer's, and Parkinson's. When you look at the symptoms of each, it is easy to see how each could be initially mistaken for the other. In my wife's case, they discovered she had them all. She went from a pillar of dependability to a frightened little girl quivering in the corner.

Alzheimer's is a chronic neurodegenerative disease that usually starts slowly and gradually worsens. It causes 60% to 70% of dementia cases.

The most common early symptom is difficulty remembering recent events, commonly called 'short-term memory loss.' As the disease advances, symptoms can include problems with language, disorientation (including easily getting lost), mood swings, loss of motivation, not managing self-care, and behavioral issues.

As a person's condition declines, they often withdraw from family and society. Gradually, bodily functions are lost, ultimately leading to death. Although the speed of progression can vary, the average life expectancy following diagnosis is three to nine years.

Dementia is a broad category of brain disease that causes a long-term and often gradual decrease in the ability to think and remember. Sometimes, it can be severe enough to affect a person's daily functioning. Other common symptoms include emotional problems, problems with language, and decreased motivation.

A person's consciousness is usually not affected. A dementia diagnosis requires a change from a person's normal mental functioning and a significant decline than one would expect due to aging. These diseases also have a substantial effect on a person's caregivers.

Parkinson's disease (PD) is a long-term degenerative disorder of the central nervous system that mainly affects the motor system. The symptoms come on slowly. Early in the disease, the most obvious are shaking, rigidity, slow movement, and difficulty walking. Thinking and behavioral problems may also occur.

Dementia becomes common in the advanced stages of the disease. Depression and anxiety are also commonly occurring in more than a third of people with PD. Other symptoms include sensory, sleep, and emotional problems. The major motor symptoms are collectively called "parkinsonism" or a "parkinsonian syndrome."

With that information explained, I'll close this prologue with a recent conversation I had with a 'friend' I ran into one day. He asked me about my wife and how she was doing. I went through her travails: the stroke and the onset of Parkinson's. Toss in a side of Alzheimer's and dementia, and you've got my life.

Then he said something I have been asked a little too frequently. "How do you deal with it?" I had to take a deep breath or two before I could answer. I had to think of how to describe my feelings and rein in my emotions to avoid crying.

I told him I would occasionally get frustrated with her but never angry. I know her slide from reality hurts her, and none of this is her intent. Throughout a lifetime, she has done more for me than I ever deserved. I am only paying her back with all the love and dignity I can find. I live for the moments when she is relatively much like the woman I fell in love with so long ago.

She sometimes is almost herself, and occasionally, she has a decent day or two in a row. I take those moments to get me through the more challenging times. Some call that crazy, but I call it the very definition of love. I remember the words I was asked to repeat way back in the mid-1970s: *'For better or for worse. In sickness and health.'* I made the promise to *'love, honor, cherish and protect her, forsaking all others.'* Your word means something, or it doesn't.

In the end, the reason we married, or at least the reason I married, was to find a partner who would ride the roller coaster of life with me. Someone who would stay with me at the top of the ride and someone to hold me when the ride was wild and then winding down. Someone to experience 'Life' with me without explaining ourselves when the trip was over.

All of those things were possible in Judy. I couldn't even fathom my life with anyone else. Judy used to say, "*I can't remember...*"

I would tell her as gently as possible, 'I remember Judy," and tell her about that part of our life.

So, by writing all this down, I remember our story for her.

Thanks for reading our story.

Regards,
Verwayne
March 2018
Revised May 2024

A Quick Note

Two things. Most of this story centers on me and what I did in my life, but the story is about my wife, and how she reacted to those situations.

Second, a beta reader asked me how we could always giggle, laugh, and kiss because *No one does that!*

I beg to differ, my friend. We were young, in love, and in jobs that saw daily trauma, life, and death. We witnessed 'crimes against humanity' in the form of murder and abuses against children, spouses, and neighbors.

It was how we coped.

We learned that by carrying on like we were kids away from our scenes, we could handle some gruesome stuff. So when you read, we laughed, giggled, and kissed with our girlfriends and, later, our wives; it was a release of pressure that worked for us.

The First Time We Met

In retrospect, I know the first time we met wasn't the time I am about to tell you. But it was the first time I remember seeing her for the beautiful woman she was. We took a course on reading EKGs at a major college near our homes.

Later, Judy told me she had only taken the course to catch my attention. I knew she was there, but I never noticed her other than being just another nurse who occasionally visited the ER while we were there.

It was strange when I look back on that day. Judy had been in the same classroom as I had been, but she was in a group of local nurses, and I was in a group of paramedics. As I recall, it was the last day of the ten-day course, and everyone in our separate groups had all met at a McDonald's restaurant just off-campus. The place was busy, and we all had to sit at one big table.

We had just sat down to eat and talk about the last test when she caught my eye. She was wearing a grayish-green dress and sandals. It was a moment that will always be clear in my mind. She was terribly shy, but still doing her best to get me to look at her. I didn't understand it then, and to this day, I still don't know why she wanted to impress me.

I was and always have been a big guy. My weight has been a problem for me since I was very young. I didn't see why a woman as beautiful as she would pay me any mind, but it suddenly occurred to me she was flirting with me. It sounds goofy, but suddenly, we were the only ones in the room. Her face was radiant, and her smile filled my eyes. If I close them right now, I can remember that smile as if it had just happened.

I gave up my seat, went over to where she was standing, and asked her if she wanted to sit outside and talk. To this day, I can clearly remember her shy smile as she nodded, and we went out the door. I can't remember what we talked about, but I told my roommate and fellow medic I would marry that girl on the way home. I later learned she had told her roommate and fellow nurse the same thing.

The ultimate irony was that her roommate and my roommate married about four months after we were married. He was my best man, and I was his. We spent a lot of time talking about *the girls* while we were on call or when we caught one of them when we delivered a patient to their hospital—just seeing her made any bad day better.

Love is goofy like that.

Moving Forward

When we left McDonald's, Judy and I agreed to 'get together' as soon as possible. It wasn't as easy as you might think. She was an OB nurse working five-midnight shifts a week, and I was a paramedic working three or four twenty-four-hour shifts a week. Our shifts wouldn't line up all too often, but she became a regular visitor at our ambulance base.

Even though she didn't enjoy working in the Emergency Medical Systems (EMS), she began to ride with us. My partner and I thought it was funny that while she was terrified of what we called *'blood, guts, hair, teeth, and eyeballs,'* you could bank on Judy showing up to ride along.

As I said, love is goofy like that.

At least four times, her OB experience made her invaluable to us. In the twelve years I was a medic, I had delivered about thirty-five babies in the field. With her aboard, we ran into two difficult impending delivery situations, and Judy was able to make the situation stable. Each time, both mom, and baby turned out just fine. Without her expertise, that might not have been the case.

Judy appealed to some hospital supervisors to align her schedule with mine, and we finally got enough time to go out on an actual date. While I had told you I was always a 'big' guy, my years in college had been good to me. I had precious few dates in high school, but college was another thing. I dated regularly and thought I had a fair idea of what made up a good date for most girls.

On the other hand, Judy had only two or three at most dates in her life. She was twenty-one when we met and had led a very sheltered social life. Outside the hospital, she had always been 'persona non grata.' Her riding along with us was a significant life experience.

At first, she was terrified by some of the scenes we encountered. After three weeks, she calmed down and used some of her medical knowledge. She even signed up for the next Advanced Red Cross First Aid class my partner and I taught.

Steve, my paramedic cohort in crime, always teased her about schmoozing one of the instructors for a better grade. Whenever he caught us holding hands, Steve would begin with his "Trying to get straight A's, huh?" pattern. It took some time, but Judy started to laugh with the rest of us.

When I finally met her parents about six weeks after we began dating, her dad was the first to pull me aside. At first, I thought I was in trouble, but he wanted to warn and compliment me about what he saw in our interactions. He 'warned' me that Judy had never had an actual boyfriend and asked that I keep that in mind.

He then complimented me on the new Judy he saw coming to life. He said that he had never seen her smile so broadly and that her entire demeanor was different. I promised him I would care for his daughter and treat her respectfully.

I told him that while my group of guys were all crazy medics, everything was always loose, and the guys were very accepting of her. I promised him I would do my best to open her to a new world.

As we returned to the rest of the family, I said I thought her smile was beautiful. He smiled at me and whispered, "Just don't hurt her." I nodded and made the little kids 'cross my heart' motion to signal my understanding.

What he had said was true. The Judy I had known before we began to date was long gone. More likely than not, a smile graced her face, her grey-blue eyes twinkled, and her gait was more assertive. Her hospital supervisor told me that dating me had made her more relaxed when she was at work, and she seemed much happier.

Oh, the things you do for love.

Our First Real Date

Several weeks passed with our dates of teaching first aid classes or making runs to a local restaurant. Steve and I talked about attending a large local county fair, and Judy asked where it was held. We were both amazed that she had never heard of it, but we also conceded that she had grown up about sixty miles north of our base. Somewhere along the line, Judy talked with her roommate, who had just started dating Steve, and the next thing I knew, we were on the way to the fairgrounds together.

I have attended this fair since I was a kid, and I have always visited the livestock barns because I grew up on a farm. By then, I was years away from working on the farm, but loved looking at the animals on display. Judy had never been around many farm animals and was full of questions about the various critters we saw.

I had steered our course to the small animal exhibits, and she loved the multiple chickens, rabbits, sheep, goats, and guinea pigs in the stacks of exhibit cages. After leaving the rabbit and small animal areas, we made our way to the cattle barns.

I pointed out the various breeds and their uses on the farm. Some were raised for milk production, some for meat production, and some for both, with a few that were strictly intended to be used for their meat. Judy had seen cattle on an uncle's farm before, but never so up close and personal. I could see she was enjoying herself.

The horse barn was next to the cattle, making our next trip a natural choice. While we had over a hundred cows on Dad's farm, we might have only had about ten horses, but one pair of them were the giant Belgian workhorses. Ours had been gentle giants, and even as a young boy, I felt no fear of them as I worked in the pasture fields with them.

The exhibit barns had several pairs of them, and it took some coaxing to make Judy realize that getting kicked by one of them was highly unlikely as long as we were quiet and didn't frighten them. I handed her a handful of fresh hay to feed them. She was nervous, but the animals knickered softly as they reached for the hay and gently took it from her hand. She was amazed by their gentleness.

Finally, we headed into the pig area. Growing up on the farm, I became well acquainted with the various smells of the animals. Then, there was the one smell anyone could pick off immediately: the smell of pigs, especially those kept in a confined area.

While the exhibitors did a good job of keeping the pens clean, they still reeked of pigs. Judy was doing her best to calm the queasy feeling in her stomach. She didn't want to make a scene. It took all I could do to keep from laughing at her. Naturally, we left that exhibit area much faster than the others.

Once outside, she pulled me closer and asked me how the people could exhibit animals that were ill. I told her I hadn't seen any animals that weren't in anything but the top shape, but she was adamant that at least two of them were sick. I asked her to show me which ones, and she agreed to go back in and point them out.

Judy had put her sweater over her mouth and nose, and we moved back to the pig barn at a pace only a nurse could keep. We quickly stopped, and she pointed out two pigs in side-by-side pens. "See what I mean? These two have tumors. Big tumors."

I looked at where she was pointing and started laughing. She couldn't understand why I found these 'sick pigs' funny. I took her hand and hustled her outside so she could breathe again, and one more time, she asked what I found so funny.

It took me a minute to stop laughing before I could finally explain that what she thought were tumors were testicles. She blushed and then told me she didn't believe me. No animal could have testicles that big. I started laughing even harder and took her back in to see them again.

As I pointed out their location on the pig's anatomy, the kid who owned them wandered in, and I asked him about his pigs. The boy was quite happy that someone would ask him about them, and he explained their age and such when I interrupted him.

"My girlfriend wanted to know if pigs at this age all have testicles of that size. Do you think these are normal for their age?" The youngster assured Judy that this was normal for pigs at this age.

I thanked him for his time and complimented him on his beautiful animals, and we left. Even in the multi-colored fairground lights, I could see Judy blushing and embarrassed. I laughed again and told her she wasn't the first or last person who didn't know about that massive bulge on the backside of a male pig.

I giggled and explained to her that her only exposure to such things was to men. I assured her that humans were no competition for pigs in that area. She finally laughed, and we went to the central fair area.

Judy saw the enormous Ferris wheel in the Midway, and of course, she wanted to ride it. I was not a big fan of the Ferris wheel and tried to weasel out of riding it. Judy pointed out that she had walked in the animal barns, and the least I could do was ride the big wheel with her. After some good-natured ribbing about being afraid, I finally agreed.

Ten minutes later, we stood in line with Judy, who threatened to make the seat rock as much as she could in return for embarrassing her about the pigs. I stood as close to her as I could and shivered. It was August, and I wasn't cold, but I felt myself falling in love with the girl who was kidding me about my fear of heights.

When we finally got on, I put my arm around her waist for the first time in our relationship, and she leaned into me. I thought I heard a sigh of happiness, but I said nothing because I was just as happy as she was. It was getting late, and the wheel operator left us circling for a good ten minutes. While I wasn't a fan of the machine, my fear was overwhelmed by the happiness I felt as Judy nestled into me.

I felt her shiver and asked if she was cold. "No, I'm fine. I'm just happy." I saw her smile and felt her sink back into my side. When we got off the wheel, I realized the girl was in love with me, leaving me wanting to cry. I didn't want her to see me cry, but I sure wanted to let the world know how I felt.

The rest of the night was spent riding some of the various attractions and buying highly overpriced food and drinks. Steve and I both had to be back on duty at eight in the morning, so we made our way back to the car. It took several more minutes to get out to the main road and head home.

Traffic was heavy until about five miles north of the event, and things calmed down. Steve's girlfriend Lois told Judy about some things they had seen, and I piped up that she should ask Judy about the sick animals she had seen. Judy swatted at me, and I started laughing.

Naturally, Steve and Lois wanted to know what I was talking about, and I explained I would tell Steve later.

I got swatted again, but I remind you one more time that love is goofy like that.

'Let's Eat In Tonight!'

A week after the fair, Judy and Lois asked Steve and me to eat at their apartment. We had always taken the girls out and thought it would be nice to be served a meal that they had made. Steve had made a wisecrack about this being a test run for a future marriage, which brought a shy smile to Judy's face.

The one thing I had made clear in advance was that I did not like onions. I had grown up near a massive onion plantation, and you could smell onions in the air every day of the year. In the summer, it was nearly unbearable to me. Especially in the summer, you could hear the giant fans that kept the onions dry and at the proper temperature twenty-four hours a day.

When we arrived, the girls showed us to their dining area and sat us down. Lois brought in our drinks, and Judy came in behind her, carrying a big plate of chicken. The first thing I noticed when I looked at the meat was that it hadn't been breaded. I looked over at Steve and saw the same trepidation on his face that I felt.

Judy sat the plate of chicken down in the center of the table and smiled. Steve finally reached across with his fork and picked up a piece, and I did the same. I cautiously took a bite and almost lost my stomach. It was barely warm, and it was borderline raw. I mustered every ounce of will I could find and managed to eat the meat.

When I finished my first piece of chicken, Lois brought out a plate of steaming hot, crunchy potato chunks. I figured I would salvage the meal with the potatoes, but as soon as I put it in my mouth, I couldn't help but spit it back out. It was the flavored onion variety.

It took me nearly a full minute to keep from vomiting up the chicken, but I finally stopped the convulsing in my stomach. I saw Judy's horrified look and Steve's nonstop laughter. He finally could talk long enough to tell Judy, "I told you he would know there were onions in those!" Then he laughed so hard that in a few seconds, we were all laughing.

The good thing about the 'onion affair' as we recalled that particular moment in the following days was that it gave me a reason not to eat a second piece of chicken. I was never a drinking man, but I was thankful when they offered me a small glass of rum and soda. I swirled it around my mouth and finally got the onion taste out of my mouth.

In the meantime, I looked up and saw Judy about ready to cry. She had made me a meal, which made me gag, and she was emotionally crushed. I got up and went over to comfort her. I pulled her in close and hugged her tight, and I felt her sobbing in my arms. I whispered, trying to soothe her, but it only made her sob even harder.

I finally got her slowed down, pushed her away long enough to look her in the eyes, and told her everything was alright. She sobbed a bit and blurted out, "You are going to hate me. I can't cook. I don't know how." Then, the tears and sobs started anew.

I held her for a few more minutes, trying to absorb her pain and her fears. I was entirely beside myself on what to do. I finally pushed her away again, took her face into my hands, and brought her forehead to mine. Tears streamed down her cheeks when I assured her I wasn't upset and that nothing would change between us.

She shook her head and whispered that I wouldn't want her because she couldn't cook. I promised she could learn and that Steve and I could teach her. While Steve and I had found the situation funny, I could see the hurt on her face. I did what I had to do. I kissed her, and she went silent.

We had held hands, and she allowed me to put my arm around her, but I had never kissed her. She had never acted like she wanted to go that far, and I had sensed a barrier of resistance when I sat next to her and pulled her against me. While she had stopped crying, I could still see the hurt on her face, so I kissed her again.

I pulled her in tight and whispered that I loved her, and she started sobbing again. I asked her if I had upset her. She lowered her face and told me that no one had ever kissed her or said 'I love you' and that she couldn't believe I meant it.

I kissed her lightly on the lips and pulled her close again. Softly and powerfully, I told her again that I loved her and that those words were nothing I would ever say if I didn't mean them. I felt her hold me closer. It was another ten minutes before she finally let go.

We turned around, expecting to see Steve and Lois, but they had politely adjourned to the porch outside. Judy washed her face and then went out to be with our friends. I stopped her, put my hands on her shoulders, and looked straight into her bluish-gray eyes. It took me a moment to gather myself, but I finally told her, "Girl, I love you. You may not believe me right now, but give me time, and I'll prove it to you."

I saw small tears welling in her eyes and wiped them away with a tissue.

Judy finally regained her composure, and we walked out onto the porch. Summer was ending, but it was a beautiful night. Despite being in town, we could hear the frogs talking along the shore of the lake bordering the village, and the crickets were singing out. When we walked out on the porch, Steve made a smart-mouth comment asking if I was still nauseous, and I laughed, assuring him that all was well.

We sat on the porch swings for about twenty minutes before Lois finally said she had to be up at 5:30 am for work. Steve and I had to be at work the next day, but we changed shifts at 8 am, a much more civilized time of the day. I gave Judy one last hug and a small kiss, trying not to attract too much attention.

Steve thanked Judy for a 'wonderful meal,' making her blush again. I squeezed her hand, and she smiled. The girls both went inside as we bid them good night. Steve jumped in to drive my new 1973 Monte Carlo, and we were soon out of the drive and on our way home. He didn't say much for most of the trip. I knew he was giving me a chance to talk first.

If I were ever to have what they used to call a *brother from another mother*, it would have been Steve. We had become so good at our jobs that we rarely had to wonder where the other guy was because we knew.

We had worked together long enough to know what we would do when we came onto the scene. We could communicate without saying a word, and on this night, Steve knew what was on my mind.

Finally, he cleared his throat and casually said, "Eventful night, huh?" We both laughed and exchanged a bit of small talk, both of us trying to avoid the apparent subject. A few minutes later, we pulled into our home's driveway. As we were getting out of the car, he stood up and put his arms on the top of the vehicle.

I smiled at him and did the same. "I see we are kissing now, huh?"

Steve had known Judy a lot longer than I had known her. They had worked together in the hospital before he became a medic. "You know Judy has been hurt several times, right?" I nodded that I knew her situation. "She's a shy girl with a sweet soul. Don't hurt her if you aren't serious about her."

We stood there a minute before I finally walked over to our house door and hugged him.

It seemed weird to others, but Steve and I were brothers in every way possible. In dangerous situations, we acted to protect each other. We had laughed and cried together over what we had seen and done in our experiences. His thoughts were my thoughts. In danger and now, in matters of love, we understood each other without saying much.

"My friend, I promise you I won't hurt her. Remember what I told you on the way home from the EKG class? I told you I was going to marry that girl. After tonight, I'm one step closer to doing just that." He took my hand and shook it, then gave me another hug.

"Judy is like a little sister to me, and I just wanted you to know that it will be slow going to get her to trust you, but she will." We walked inside and sat down in our chairs to watch the news.

"V?" I looked at him, waiting for his question. "I'm glad you will be the one to bring her out of her shell. Give her the time to build her confidence, and you'll be amazed at what will bloom."

I smiled. We didn't have to talk. We just understood each other.

I thought about that night many times. It could have gone wrong, but things were made right. Many nights, we would talk about the 'onion affair,' which became the source of hours of laughter between us.

I remembered it as the start of the caterpillar escaping its cocoon, and Judy remembered it as the night of her first proper kiss. We both remembered it as the start of something good.

Walking On Sunshine

The next few weeks were wonderful days for us. Everyone saw a new kick in Judy's step and a bigger smile. While my original intention was to make her understand what she meant to me, it gave her an entirely new outlook on life. She was still shy, but she was no longer hiding in the background in a group. That I had given her proper recognition as a woman had made her much more confident.

One morning, she had agreed to meet me at a local restaurant for breakfast before she went home to sleep, and I reported to work at the ambulance base. It was always a short time of just us together, but it was a time we both looked forward to spending together. We usually had coffee and a donut or something along those lines, giving us a chance to hold hands.

As I was getting ready to leave my house to meet her, the phone rang, and I thought I was being called in early. I was the base supervisor, and that happened a lot. Instead, it was Judy's nursing supervisor. She laughed after asking if she had awakened me, and I told her I was already up and about out the door.

"I wanted to compliment you on what you are doing for Judy. Whatever it might be, she is a completely different person." I had known this lady for a long time. I explained all I had done was give her confidence by telling her I loved her.

"That will do it!" she replied. Judy was always quiet, but now she is just bubbling." I thanked her for calling me and headed out the door.

I usually arrived at the restaurant because it was only about two miles from my home and fifteen miles from the hospital where Judy worked. I walked in the door and looked around for her. One of the waitresses who knew me pointed to the back corner of the dining area, telling me she was way back in the corner. I thanked her and made my way to the back.

We sat side by side, mainly so I could hold her hand without leaning forward. Judy told me about her night and her upcoming schedule. I usually did most of the talking, but this particular morning, she was a chatterbox. I smiled, and she stopped talking for a minute. After a moment, she asked me, "Why are you looking at me that way?"

"Well, dear lady, everyone from the hospital is asking me what I did to you to make you smile so much lately. I've told them all that, just like in fairy tales, where the princess is awakened with a kiss. I kissed you, and you seemed to smile more and act happier. They tell me you are acting so much happier than you normally do, and I told them it had to be that kiss."

Instead of laughing, I could see her trying to figure out how she wanted to respond. For a moment, I was afraid I had upset her applecart, a phrase my Dad had always used. I was about to apologize for my words when she talked again.

"I always heard girls say that they felt like they were walking on air when they fell in love with the right guy. I never believed that until it happened to me." Her eyes looked straight into mine with an intensity most people can't seem to find. "You see, now I know why it happens. Since that night, when you kissed me and said those three words, my heart has taken on wings, and my feet are dancing. It does feel like I am walking on air."

I've heard profound words before, but those words, spoken some forty-five years ago, still strike me as some of the most profound concepts of my life. I've always said,' Some people spend their lives waiting for things that will never happen.' Judy was becoming aware that something she hadn't expected to occur had finally come to her.

It was rapidly closing in on the time I had to report for duty, and we left the restaurant and made our way to the parking lot. I hugged her and whispered,'I love you!' in her ear. As I pulled back, I kissed her on the cheek. I saw her smile broaden as she pulled away from me and got into her car. I whispered, 'I love you!' again and watched her head home to sleep for the rest of the day.

As I drove to work, I realized that Judy's feet were not the only ones not touching the ground. Although our relationship was still very young, I could tell the Spinners were right; we might have one of those 'One of Kind Love Affairs.'

Love Is In The Air

As the weeks and months went by, our relationship grew stronger. Yes, we had the occasional disagreement. You wouldn't be truthful or human if you tried to tell me you have never disagreed with your 'significant other.' We had disagreed on occasions, but one of the things that my father said to me as he watched the two of us grow closer was to weigh my options.

"If you love this girl, is it worth arguing over some small thing and ruining everything, or would it be easier to compromise and meet her idea with one of yours? In the long run, if it isn't worth fighting about, isn't it easier to say, 'Yes, dear,' and find another way to do things?"

Of course, he was right. Dad had long been my 'go-to' guy for advice all my life, even about matters of love.

The first time I implemented the 'yes dear' policy was about something small. I think it was about which movie to watch. I didn't want to see the film Judy wanted to see and told her so. She told me she had been waiting to see that particular movie, and that night might be the last one she would have off before it left town.

I almost opened my mouth again when I remembered Dad's words. *'Is it worth fighting about?'* It was not, and I agreed, and we went to her show. It wasn't as bad as I thought it might have been, and she was happier for being able to go to her movie.

Over the years, we learned that compromise was always more comfortable than fighting. Again, we had disagreements, sometimes heated disputes, but one of us eventually realized what Dad had taught me. *'Is it worth it?'* After all, we were young, and our lives were just getting started.

After just such a statement, Judy rode with us on an accident call that was one of the most devastating of my career, involving two cars driven by teenagers. Two kids were dead at the scene, and we fought to save the lives of three others heading to a major trauma center. They were bleeding heavily and had sustained terrible fractures.

In the end, one of the girls died in surgery, but the other two boys lived. As we were cleaning up our ambulance rig, the mother of one of the children arrived at the hospital and was told that her child was in surgery. There are very few things that will move you, like listening to a mother sob as she said to no one in particular that their last words to each other were '*I hate you!*'

"He was mad I wouldn't lend him twenty dollars for something, and as he went out the door, he yelled out, '*I hate you!*'" She sobbed loudly and uncontrollably for a moment before regaining herself. "Before he got out the door, I yelled back, '*Well, I hate you too!*' I want to take those words back! I love my son. I was just upset with him. *I love my son!* **Please**, I love my son!"

I have heard those words too many times in my life, and while you can understand the agony, you never get used to it. I took a few minutes to talk with her in a quieter hallway. I explained that while I had no way of knowing how he would turn out, her son was the least injured of the three. It was of little consolation to her then, but about ten minutes later, one of the surgery nurses came out to tell her that her son was in the recovery room and escorted her back to see him.

On the way home, I could see that Judy was upset. The mother's crying about her words to her son had shaken her deeply. We talked about the accident scene, what we might have done differently, and how the accident might have occurred—all typical conversations for Steve and me.

As we drew closer to our base, Judy asked how anyone could tell their child they hate them. Steve told her, "Most parents would never say such a thing, and most children would never say it to a parent. Emotions can cause people to do or say things they don't mean."

Judy had never been exposed to that type of behavior and didn't understand it. Steve told her that many things we run into routinely make little sense, yet they happen. People say things they don't mean, especially when they are upset.

On our next date alone, I learned how much the emergency room scene had affected her. As we drove along, Judy said to me, "Let's agree right now to never say the words, '*I hate you.*' I don't care how mad you ever get with me, or I get with you; let's never say those words." She reached for my right hand from the steering wheel, and I gave it to her. Her grip told me she was quite serious.

I asked her what had brought her to ask me about this subject, knowing full well why we were going to talk about it. "All night at work, all I could remember was how that lady cried there in the ER. Her sobs struck my heart so deeply that I dreamed about her. I don't ever want to be like her. I never want to hold that regret for the rest of my lifetime. I don't. *I can't*. I could never live after something like that."

I understood what she was telling me. I had seen others cry and say similar words after a tragedy, which touched me every time. You can get used to the gore, at least to the point where you don't have nightmares about it. But you never get used to the emotions you feel after those situations.

I always told new people coming in to volunteer at our base or those new hires who had never been on such a tragedy. You can't allow the things you see to get to you or that you are done as a medic. Put it away mentally, keep going, and unpack it later. It was the only way you could do the job.

"Promise me you'll never say those words to me." As best I could while driving, I looked into her eyes. I saw the small tears forming in her eyes and felt her squeeze my hand even harder. "Let's never get that angry with each other. Promise me."

At about that time, we arrived at our destination. I parked the car, shut the engine down, and turned to face her. "Judy, I promise you I will never say those words to you. I promise that no matter what happens during the day, I will always close the day by telling you I love you. Every night, every day. I'll tell you so often that you'll grow tired of hearing it because I do love you, and that is forever."

She leaned toward me, and as best as we could in the car, she hugged me.

As our time that night wore down and I was dropping her off at her apartment, I whispered in her ear, "I love you," and she smiled. "You see that it's worth telling you that just to see that smile." She got out of the car and headed toward her door. I got out and caught up with her, and she asked me if I had forgotten something. I told her she was the one who had forgotten something.

I could see her trying to remember what she had forgotten. I reached in and kissed her cheek, and her eyes lit up. "Oh, yes! I love you!" I kissed her again and then headed back to the car and home. That night began a custom we carried on for nearly forty-five years. We said those three words every time we parted, even for a few minutes. We said those three words every phone call, every night, and every morning.

It became a habit, but was far more than a habit. It was a statement of truth. We both had seen that life is not assured — not next year, next week, or even the next minute. You are not promised anything. Our emergency runs together had shown us that. You could be driving down the road one second and hit by a truck two seconds later. You just never knew when something might happen.

From a tragedy, we learned to express our love to one another. A friend of mine once told me, "I think I heard you tell your wife today, 'I love you' more than I have told my wife that in over a month!" I explained to him it reflected more on him than it ever did on me. It took him back a little, but he caught on to what I meant.

"You see if I were to die before I get home again, Judy would always remember that our last words to one another were, 'I love you.' Wouldn't that be comforting for her to know?" He slowly nodded. I didn't spend much time with that man, but when I did, I realized he was saying those three words to his wife much more often. Now and then, I would hear her say them back to him.

It was a constant in our lives. It cost us nothing but meant so much to both of us. Over the years, we spent a lot of time on the road in large cities. We expanded the pact to include that we would call one another after arriving at our respective destinations to say those three words.

It was a habit that became an obsession. It was that important to us.

Secrets of Long Ago

As time is prone to do, summer became fall, and winter arrived four days before Christmas. I was looking forward to spending a few days with Judy without worrying about schedules and such. We had both taken mini-vacations, although we had no plans beyond being with each other. Our relationship had become tight, and I couldn't fathom being with anyone other than Judy.

We had plans to attend my family's Christmas get-together one day and then drive the seventy-some miles the other way to spend the day before Christmas Eve with hers. We both had volunteered to work Christmas Eve and Christmas to give our fellow workers with children the holidays off.

Judy's roommate had plans to be away, and my roommate was going with her, so we decided Judy could spend those days at our place. We naturally collected a lot of harassment about those 'sleeping' arrangements, but Steve knew I was well aware of Judy's fears. She had been hurt in two other relationships that had gone bad in a hurry after getting off to a good start. He knew I valued her love too much to hurt her.

When we were finally alone, we spent hours talking about things like my childhood, Judy's childhood, and our hopes and aspirations. It was a beautiful day. We made ourselves something to eat and sat down to watch television and talk more. I couldn't remember a time when Judy had seemed happier.

When we were too tired to talk anymore, I showed her the room we had set up for her. She kissed me, told me she loved me and went into the bedroom. I went to my bedroom and wasted no time falling asleep. My eyes were heavy, but my heart was singing. I was happy.

I was in the middle of a dream, walking down a trail in a nearby wood with Judy, when my door swung open. I was startled awake and strained to see what had happened. It took a moment, but I realized Judy was standing at the door, looking at me. "What's wrong, dear?" I had heard that she was prone to sleepwalking, but as she stepped toward me, I knew she was awake.

I flipped my bedside lamp on, and she sat down on the bed beside me. "I can't sleep. I can't stop thinking about today. Would you mind if I were to lie down beside you?" While I most certainly welcomed her, that little voice in my mind told me to proceed carefully. I slid closer to the wall and motioned her to climb in with me.

As she adjusted herself in the bed and then adjusted her nightgown, I made sure that she had all the space she needed to feel comfortable yet safe. "Thank you. I didn't want to be alone." I told her she was safe with me. Judy talked a bit before falling silent, and I thought she was asleep.

About five minutes after she stopped wiggling, and I was falling back to sleep, Judy reached over and pulled my arm around her waist. She snuggled in closer to me. I heard a small sigh escape her and then nothing. I used my arm to grasp her closer, hoping to give her some security.

A few moments later, I thought I heard her begin to snore and relax a bit. Then I felt a shudder from her, followed by another. Just as I was about to ask her if she was alright, she broke out in a series of deep sobs and then a flood of tears. I was bewildered, thinking that perhaps I had touched her the wrong way.

It took me about two minutes to get her to turn around to face me and apologize for whatever I had done to make her cry. My words seemed to make her sob all the more, so I just held her and waited. I didn't know what else I could do for her.

Several minutes passed before her crying eased up, and she attempted to tell me something. Her words came haltingly initially, but it was like a bursting dam gushing forth once they started. She told me of a 'sin' she had committed long ago, and as she said it, my stomach quivered as I felt the forlornness in her voice.

"He told me he had a new color TV and wanted to show it to me. He said he had a color TV. He kissed me all over, and then..."

Another spasm of sobs covered her words before she was able to continue. "He began to touch me. He put his hand up my dress and felt my leg. *I couldn't stop him. He said he had a new color TV!*"

I stopped her and held her as close to me as I could. "Shhhhh, Judy. It's alright. I promise that it's alright." Her body shuddered violently against me, and her sobs filled my ear. I tried to hold her close enough to absorb her pain and her fears, but the tighter I held her, the more she cried. I felt utterly useless.

We stayed like that for nearly an hour. Judy's body was shuddering against mine; her sobs were echoing in my head. Her tears had soaked my T-shirt, and I could feel them running down my chest. I said nothing and did nothing except to be there for her.

When Judy finally spoke again, she told me about a time when she was almost ten, and her family had attended a Christmas party with some friends. One of the older men there had cornered her and told her about his brand-new color television at his place, just down the road. He told her that if she wanted, he would be glad to take her down there so she could see how beautiful the programs were in color.

Color television had just become affordable in the early 1960s for those not my age, and only the well-off could afford one. Judy had seen one in the local hardware store window but had never seen one up close, so she jumped at the chance. He warned her they had to be quiet as they left, or all the other kids would want to go with them, and he didn't want a bunch of kids in his expensive new house.

Naturally, she was as stealthy as a young girl as they slipped out the door. He turned the television on and sat her on his lap as they waited for it to warm up and come into view. She was watching a cereal commercial when his hand found its way to her knee and slipped up along her thigh.

He pulled her close, kissed her, and pushed his hand higher, but about the time his hand started its second advance, and she began to shriek.

He stopped and began to quiet her, but his luck then was about the same as mine that night. Judy said she cried for a good twenty minutes before he got her to stop. He washed her face with a cold cloth and gave her a small bag of Christmas candy to buy her silence. He got her in the car, and she rode back to the party with a stone-faced stare. Once inside, he whispered to her not to say anything to anyone, and within minutes, he was gone.

I tried to interrupt her, but it was like she had to get her words out. She had to tell someone. Until the story was complete, there would be no silencing her again. She told me how she had told her grandmother and was promptly told to 'stop telling stories.' Once they got home, she told her mother and got no response other than, 'You'll be alright.'

A dozen years later, I was the one left to pick up the pieces.

I explained to her that her ordeal was well behind her and that she was safe with me. To my surprise, my words set her off into another crying jag. She finally could whisper that she was afraid I wouldn't want her because of what had happened that day.

I couldn't hold myself back anymore, and my tears began to fall. "Judy, nothing in your past can stop me from loving you. Nothing. You are the sweetest lady I've ever met. Something that some nasty old man tried with you when you were a child could never change my feelings for you now."

Neither of us got much sleep that night. We went out onto the couch to sit, my arm around her shoulder. Judy told me that while nothing had happened other than some inappropriate touching, it shamed her deeply. She used the term *damaged goods* to describe herself, and I assured her over and over that she was a gem that I would treasure forever.

I suppose that if you have thought yourself 'damaged' for more than half of your life, it's difficult to change your mind in just one night.

Over the next forty-some years, her fears would break out again, and we would have to talk about it for a while. She never could enjoy Christmas with any enthusiasm, even though it was my favorite day of the year. I did my best to support her, and she did her best not to 'ruin my holiday.'

We didn't go to either of our family's Christmases. We just sat and talked until her words ran out. More than she was worried that her nightmare would scare me away, I was afraid that it would scare her away.

The day our vacation days had run out, I hugged her and whispered that I would love her forever. Come hell or high water, and nothing could change that fact.

As she walked away, she gave me a quick glimpse of that smile I grew to love so much, and I knew everything would be alright.

We Travel Across America

During a mid-winter get-together, our group of friends got talking about making a group trip to Vegas by bus. Everyone was going to get a ten-day vacation in mid-July, and we would be off to see the world—or so they thought. Of the original group of sixteen people, one week before the scheduled trip, the only two people on the journey were Judy and me. Everyone had 'something come up.'

As our last days of work counted down, I met Judy in the ER after an overdose run, and I asked her if she still wanted to go. I had traveled extensively as a kid, but she had never been out of Michigan except for a trip to an amusement park in northeastern Ohio. Without a moment's hesitation, she told me, "I can't wait! I don't care if it comes down to me and you. I want to go!" And so we went.

I remember cleaning out and packing my 1973 Monte Carlo and telling everyone we would call them now and then. Everyone who had committed to going on this trip stood on the porch to send us off. They all waved at us as we left the drive and headed out on our grand adventure. One of the original planners of the trip gave us a reservation number for a two-day stay at a nice hotel in Vegas, and we couldn't wait.

We headed north, crossed the "Mighty Mac," or the Mackinaw Bridge, turned westbound on US-2, and headed toward Vegas. We had no set plan; we just knew we didn't have to return for two weeks. Both of us had gotten sixteen days off, and we wanted to make them memorable.

We crossed Wisconsin during the night, avoiding several deer that seemed intent on cutting our trip short, and entered Minnesota as the sun began to rise. As much as I thought we had talked about things, our conversations never slowed. Judy was driving and telling me about her grandmother's outhouse, and she cut off a semi without realizing what she was doing.

There was a railroad crossing with signs telling particular trucks to stop at the tracks. The semi-truck in front of us slowed to a stop, so Judy assumed the truck in the other lane would do the same. She changed lanes in front of him, only to hear him struggling to stop without rear-ending us.

The big rig driver was unhappy about that move and slammed on the brakes. A massive cloud of smoke emerged as his tires struggled to catch traction. Somehow, he got slowed enough to avoid hitting us, and I told Judy to get moving and get back into the proper lane.

She was embarrassed at the situation but resumed driving at the speed limit. I was just getting settled back into our routine when I saw the semi coming. He was initially in the passing lane, and he was coming fast—extremely fast. It didn't take a genius to realize that he was mad.

I had Judy pick up her speed as the truck pulled in behind her. He pulled within ten feet of our bumper and kept blowing his horn. She asked me if we should pull over, and I told her there was no way I would talk with that guy. We just kept picking up speed, and he stayed behind us.

I think we crossed Minnesota at about 100 miles per hour with a fully loaded semi drafting behind us. The only thing in our favor was as soon as we crossed into North Dakota, he had to stop at an inspection center. We had been fortunate in that I had just filled the gas tank. As things resumed to normal, I explained what she had done wrong. Judy had never driven much on the various highway systems and was getting schooled.

My original plan was to go through North Dakota and into Montana. Judy was afraid that the truck driver would get through his business at his pull-off and come hunting us again. We found a rest area, and after some conversation, we turned towards South Dakota and searched the map for the route to see Mt. Rushmore. Once I had found the best course, we were off again.

We found the Mt. Rushmore monument and marveled at its wonder. We were going to leave, but realized we had parked in a small shade area and napped for a while. While we had a lot of time, we had little money to waste on fancy hotels. The Monte Carlo had seats that leaned back nicely, and we were able to catch a couple of hours of much-needed rest.

Once back out on the road, we headed to Salt Lake City and went swimming in the Great Salt Lake. It was an incredible experience. The lake is enormous, but it is quite shallow, and we walked out quite a distance.

After we were done swimming, we took advantage of the multitude of 'hose down' areas to remove the salt from our bodies. A few miles away, we found a small stream along the road and waded for a few minutes to finish the job.

To make the long trip safely, one of us would sleep while the other drove. We drove across northern Nevada into California along I-80 into Sacramento and eventually made it to San Francisco. Judy saw a sign for Fisherman's Wharf, so we headed there. It was fun to watch her look about and smile. She had never been far from home, so this was new for her.

After playing around on the Wharf, we drove along some of the city's streets. Then, we rode on one of the cable cars and crossed the Golden Gate Bridge twice. On the north end of the bridge, there was a vast hollowed-out tree large enough for an adult to stand up in its center. As I recall, these trees were part of the aftereffect of a 1964 flood.

Judy made the mistake of walking in a bit too far so that she couldn't back out without making her backside part of the scenery. Of course, I used her predicament to get a lovely photo of her putting her best side forward. As I recall, she hit me for taking that photo, but it was all part of the game that couples played.

Now, I said we crossed the Golden Gate twice in our car. We headed back south, and due to some poor planning on my part, I missed my exit to our next destination. We turned around, and again, I missed it because the traffic was too heavy to get in the proper lane.

We ended up on the north side of the bridge again. Once I got situated, I headed south one more time and immediately got into the proper lane. Finally, we were able to get off and proceed south. I caught a lot of grief from Judy, mainly because I took the photo of her backside, but we had fun. We had traveled a long way, and it was nice to be able to laugh.

We headed along the Pacific coast past Monterey along California Route 1 in total awe of the magnificent scenery. The sun was making its way toward the ocean, and we decided we needed to rest. We had driven shy of three thousand miles without much sleep and knew we couldn't continue much longer.

Keep in mind that this was the early 1970s when we came to an exit for Big Sur. We pulled off, parked along the edge, got out to use the facilities, and walked along the ocean. The place was virtually deserted, and we locked the doors on the car and got some sleep. The view of the sea from the sandy beach was incredible, but our bodies were dead tired, and we were soon fast asleep.

I'm not exactly sure why or what woke me up, but I suddenly sat up in my car seat, trying to figure out what made the noise that seemed to get closer and closer to us. I opened the door and realized the sound was coming from the incoming tide. There was no moon outside, so I turned the headlights on, and to my horror, I saw the ocean was mere feet from my front bumper.

I started the car and almost got stuck in the sand, but I finally backed out to a paved area and got out. When I walked to where we had parked, the ocean had reclaimed the sand where we had been. It was a mistake of ignorance and almost a costly and or fatal situation.

I decided I was adequately rested to drive again, and we headed south towards Los Angeles. It was a long drive, and we were tired when we arrived. I'm not exactly sure how we got there, but we ended up in Santa Ana. As we tried to figure out what to do next, Judy spotted a nice-looking hotel with a rate posted outside that I figured we could afford and got a room.

I tried to get a room with two beds, but they were out of those, leaving me to take the one-bedroom. Once again, I found myself playing the game that new couples play. Fully aware of Judy's past, once in the room, I took several blankets and a couple of pillows and made myself a place to sleep on the floor. It wasn't comfortable, but I had spent a lot of time camping, so not that bad either.

Looking back, it was funny how we danced around the situation we faced in that room. I had long been a fan of Dorothy Parker and laughed about how our position was strongly reminiscent of her 1931 story, 'Here We Are.' She wrote about a young, newly married couple on their way to their first night as a married couple.

We both showered and then headed downstairs to a small cafe in the hotel. We sat there for almost an hour, watching the foot traffic go by the windows before finally heading back to our room.

After we watched the local weather report and a couple of other programs, I stood up and told Judy, "Dear, I'm tired. I love you. I hope you sleep well." I walked over to the mattress I had made for myself and lay down. A few minutes later, she lay down for the night in the bed.

Several years later, Judy told me she desperately wanted me to lie beside her. She wanted me there but was scared that it would happen. I had decided that Judy would be the one to decide when it was time for something to happen. Some things are worth the wait.

We spent a couple of days in that hotel while visiting several of the local attractions. I had been to southern California as a teenager in 1966. I told Judy about my Disney, Sea World, and Knott's Berry Farm trips. Naturally, she wanted to visit them as well. Our first day trip was to visit Disney, and the second day was split between the other two attractions.

With each passing hour, I saw more and more of the beautiful person who lay beneath her quiet demeanor. I can remember the first time I heard her giggle as I dropped my ice cream cone at the Berry Farm. I had never heard her laugh like that before.

Later in the day, I remember Judy reaching to hold my hand as we walked out the gates toward the parking lot as naturally as you please. It was the first time that she had done such a thing. I saw it as a step toward dropping her defenses and beginning to trust me. It was a wonderful day.

The next day, we packed up and made one last trip through some of the more elegant streets in Hollywood and Los Angeles. We had a couple of hours to kill before heading to Vegas, where two nights in a high-end hotel awaited us. I wasn't much for gambling, but I had found some other attractions I thought we would enjoy together.

The drive across California toward 'Sin City' was hot. July weather at home was one thing, but July weather in the desert was a completely different creature. Fortunately, the cooling system on my car was well-maintained, and while we saw many other out-of-state vehicles sitting along the road, we were able to sail across the endless sand.

As we pulled into Vegas, I remembered the route I needed to take to get to our hotel. I hadn't wanted to run the air conditioning in the heat, and both of us desperately needed a shower and a place to rest to cool off again. My shirt was like a sponge that had fallen into the bathtub. All I could dream about was taking a shower.

We debated taking all the luggage in, but we decided only to take in our personal bag so we could rest a bit before wrestling the bags in. I walked toward the check-in area, and when I gave the lady my name and reservation number, she looked at her books and frowned. I knew right then that something was wrong.

"I'm sorry, Mr. Greenhoe, but the check we received bounced, and your reservation has been canceled."

Judy shook her head and pulled me toward the seating in the check-in area. I was about to say something when she blurted out, "I'm sorry, I knew Mike was having money troubles. They repossessed his car just before we left, and I think he was about to be evicted from his apartment. I should have known. I'm sorry."

She must have thought me crazy as I laughed. "It's alright. It's not your fault, but we'll be alright." I explained I had brought a small tent, and that I had seen a camping area outside the city and could go back there for the night. Right about then, Judy knew I was crazy.

I saw the look in her eyes as I laid out my plan, and I knew she wasn't wild about sleeping in the desert.

"Here's what we are going to do. I saw some large restrooms back there, so we can go in and wash up. That will at least cut down on the odor in the car. After that, we can put our bags back in the car and walk around the hotel. They've got a lot of things we can do for no charge so that we can cool off. What do you think?"

Judy sat there looking at me and then looking around the hotel. Finally, she agreed, and we found the bathrooms and got as clean as possible using a bathroom sink. I let her stay in the lobby as I ran the bags back to the car. When I returned, I had to return to the bathroom to wipe the sweat off my face and armpits.

We wandered about the hotel and watched some people play the slots that populated the lobby. When we found a restaurant that wasn't too busy, we went in and had a nice dinner at a reasonable price. As I remember, we sat at our table for almost two hours and talked. Instead of being the disaster we thought the situation might have been, we spent more time getting to know each other.

For maybe only the third or fourth time together, I told her, "My father always told me you need to make the best of every situation. Everyone else would have tossed a fit about this. Yes, Mike has our money, but we can deal with that later. When you get home, instead of crying about this night, you can tell your friends about the night we camped in the desert."

I watched her face for a moment, and suddenly, I was reassured that I was with the right woman. Judy smiled and began that silly little giggle, reaching for my hand and squeezing it tight. We stood up, used the restrooms again, and headed to the campground.

The one thing I knew about the desert was that the temperatures would drop. The guy at the check-in desk gave us a small tarp to put on the ground to keep away the creepy-crawly things that live there. It didn't take long to set up our tent. I was confident I'd hear something from Judy about the man's reference to the night creatures, but she said nothing.

As the night descended, we sat on a cement bench just down from our campsite and talked. In the background, the air was filled with the sounds of wild dogs, or maybe they were coyotes. It didn't matter just then. The crickets and bugs sang to us, making the night memorable for us.

I don't know when we finally crawled into the tent, but we zipped it up as tight as possible. We lay on the pile of blankets serving as our mattress, and both stripped down to our underwear to avoid sweating through everything we owned. The tent was small, and there was no way we could avoid touching each other.

I wasn't sure how Judy was going to react to the situation for a moment. I lay on my right side and faced her to minimize our skin contact. As much as I wanted to be with her, I also knew that if I made one wrong move, it could have set our relationship back months or maybe even ruined it. A sweat-fest in a tent in the middle of a desert was not worth losing the sweetest woman I had ever known.

I was tired, and just as I was about to give her a small goodnight kiss, Judy leaned into me and hugged me tightly. I wasn't prepared for her actions. She kissed me more passionately than we had ever done before. I'm not sure why; well, actually, I know why, but I ran my hand down her back to her hip and pulled her even closer to me. Instead of pulling back, her embrace became tighter.

Her response almost kicked in that primal urge that rages in most men. It was the words my father had told me in my senior year in high school came back to mind. *'Never give in to a spur-of-the-moment experience you might regret later.'* As gently as I could, I pushed back and kissed her forehead.

Judy looked at me and asked, "Did I do something wrong?" I saw her face fill with self-doubt.

"Sweetheart, you have done everything right. I would love to continue with you, but this is nowhere to go down that road. There will be better places at more appropriate times in the future. Let's wait. We have nothing but time together in our lives." I kissed her lips softly and waited for her response.

I wasn't sure how she would react. I feared I might end up with a girl-friend crying all night in a tiny tent in a scorching desert some twenty-five hundred miles from home. The last thing I expected was what she said next. "I have had such a wonderful time with you on this trip, and I felt I owed you this. I don't want to disappoint you!"

Despite the heat, I hugged her close again before pushing her back. "You never have to worry about owing me anything. I am thankful you have put your trust in me and embarked on a two-week journey with me." I stroked her face for a minute before continuing. "You are a wonderful person and a beautiful woman. If this situation presents itself at a better place and time, I will consider it an honor to be with you, but you will never 'owe' me anything."

Until this very moment, I have told no one about that night. Many memories were made in a tent in a desert just outside Vegas. Some guys would have thought me crazy, and some gals might have never considered a guy would stop them in the same situation.

I had already decided that I wanted more than just physical love from Judy. It was the Seventies, and girls who would have sex with nearly anyone were all over the place. But the girls who made me feel the way I felt when I was with Judy were years apart.

In retrospect, this trip put proposing to Judy in my brain. We had seen so much together and would spend just shy of ten thousand miles together without a single spat in some sweltering weather. It told me that what I had known the first time I had met her was accurate. This woman was an extraordinary human being.

I wanted to marry this girl who had bloomed into a beautiful woman in our few months together. I could have never asked for anything more from her as she slowly emerged from her shell. Something inside me knew she was the one I wanted to spend the rest of my days with. All I had to do was work up the courage to do it.

We left the next morning, and oddly enough, neither of us said a word about what had nearly happened the night before, but the relationship had changed. There was no longer a need to be walking someplace to hold hands. We did it in the car as well. Those three words, 'I love you!' flowed much smoother, and we didn't care who heard us say it.

We were near the 'Four Corners' area, the only place in America where four states converge at one point. We took pictures of us standing in a different state with our hands and feet.

A few minutes later, we swung south to visit the Grand Canyon and then the Hoover Dam. It was 110 degrees at the state line, and Judy laughed about how we dragged ourselves while the older folks scooted about the area like kids.

We headed back north and east to home with our vacation time winding down. The trip was uneventful, and we made better time than I had thought we would. I asked Judy if she wanted to stop in Chicago for a couple of days. I wanted to show her some of my favorite places from my younger days, namely the Museum of Science and Industry and the Museum of Natural History.

Of course, right next to the Natural History Museum were the Adler Planetarium and Shedd's Aquarium. We found an inexpensive hotel just outside Chicago and took a bus to the attractions, allowing us more time to talk. Our days in the city were fun-filled, and our night in the hotel was not a repeat of the night in the desert, although it could have been.

Years later, Judy asked me about that night in particular and why I hadn't pressed the issue, and I told her I loved and respected her too much. It sounds cliché, but it was the truth.

I realized we would have a lifetime together, leaving plenty of time for those things. Just then, it was more important for me to become better friends and get to know each other without crossing that line. I still consider it to have been one of the smartest things I ever did.

Home was still another four hours from Chicago, and to our surprise, eight of our friends were gathered when we pulled into the driveway. This event was long before the days of cell phones, but I had used a payphone to call Steve to give him an idea of when we would be home.

Everyone was there except Mike, the guy who had scammed us on the hotel deal. He had lost his job and moved away. I never worried about that money because sleeping in the desert had brought us to a new level in our relationship. In my mind, I owed Mike something for sealing a relationship that was coming into its own.

The group had a pretty elaborate dinner set up for us, and neither Judy nor I could figure out why they had set it up. Then the girls asked Judy to show them her ring, leaving her looking at them in confusion. Then Lois blurted out, "You guys didn't get married in Vegas?" It seems that everyone around us had figured that when the two of us had left, we would get married while we were in Vegas.

"Now, why would we get married in Las Vegas? I don't even like him anymore!" She laughed as everyone's mouth dropped open at her words. "Just kidding. We aren't close like that. Not even close to anything like that."

I could see the looks of disbelief as we ate, but there was when Steve and I were alone, and he whispered to me, "Your lady isn't a good liar. You guys ain't fooling anyone!" I just smiled. It had been a long time since I had been that happy.

Family Things

A hot July turned into an even hotter August that summer, and just like the weather, our romance simmered. Judy had fixed her work schedule to correspond with mine, giving us the most time together. We went shopping, paid bills, and just plain hung out together.

Probably sensing that we were about to go the next step, Judy took me to meet more of her family. She had taken me to meet her grandmothers and various aunts and uncles, but she also wanted me to meet her cousins and distant relatives.

One weekend that we both had off, her family held a huge family get-together on the backside of a large lake. Judy was delighted to introduce me to everyone, smiling all day long. She later told me that some of her kin had never really thought that she would ever have a serious boyfriend.

I enjoyed the time with her and did my best to remember everyone's name. Her grandmothers took extra time talking with me, probably to see what I was up to dating their granddaughter. They were delightful ladies, and I always looked forward to visiting them at their homes for several years. They were as different as could be imagined, but they were both a fountain of information on family history.

Likewise, I took Judy to meet my dad and family whenever possible. I can still remember the smile I saw on my dad's face when he first met Judy. Dad was the kind of person who could talk to anyone, but he took a genuine interest in Judy. I was almost jealous as they spoke and all but forgot everyone else in the room.

The next time I talked with Dad without her, I asked him what he had thought about her. He just sat in his chair and smiled a goofy smile. He had a way of doing that kind of thing to me. When I finally got him to talk about her, he told me that if I wanted to keep her, I needed to snatch her up as fast as possible. "You need to do something soon before you lose her to someone who wasn't dragging their feet."

"So, you like her?" I had to know.

Since I was young, my father called me Doc due to my interest in medical things. True to form, he started out using that nickname. "Doc, it doesn't take much of a genius to see that you've found a special lady. I've met a lot of your girlfriends, and I have never seen the look I see on your face now. It's even easier to see when you are with her. If you want to be happy for the rest of your life, make your move soon before someone else grabs her."

We lived much closer to my dad than we were to her family, and we spent more time at Dad's place. Every time I brought her with me, Dad would talk with Judy more than anyone else who was there. I remember the day my sister told me, "I think Dad likes her more than he likes us!"

She was right. My Father was obviously taken with Judy, and they could spend hours talking to one another. Having seen a lot of families who didn't like their children's spousal choices, I was delighted to see my family become so close to Judy. However, there came a day when that bond was severely tested.

My dad was a voracious coffee drinker, capable of drinking twenty or more cups a day. He took his coffee black and would chide me for adding cream and sugar to mine. "One of these days, Doc, you'll grow up and drink your coffee like a man." Dad had never had more than one coffee cup for over a decade and never washed it. When he left the house, he would rinse it and set it upside down to dry.

The outside had taken on a light tan hue, but the inside was a deep gold color. Everyone in the family knew that you didn't wash or even touch that cup, but somehow, I forgot to tell Judy.

We were there in late August, and Dad asked me to help him in the garage. He loved tinkering with the old 'hit and miss drip engines' from the 1890s era. He had one he wanted to move from one side of the garage to the other. Dad told me he was about to finish rebuilding it and tried to get it closer to the contraption he had built to hold it still when he fired it.

Dad, my brother, and I finally got it where he wanted it. We came in and went to the sink to wash up. Right there on a towel sat Dad's coffee cup, now a shiny white, and it reeked of bleach. I looked over at Judy, and she was beaming with pride. I was about to ask her what she had done, but she beat me to it.

"I saw how dirty your cup was, so I washed it! It took quite a bit of scrubbing to clean it, but it's white again."

My brother had gone pale, and I was trying not to cry, but with nary a skip in his step, Dad walked over to her, hugged her, and said, 'Thank you.' He took the cup to the sink, rinsed it again, and poured himself a cup of coffee, leaving my brother and me speechless. Seeing him wince as he drank from it took a subtle eye, but he said nothing to Judy.

Naturally, for the next few years, Judy learned she had done a naughty thing by washing his cup. But Dad just laughed about it and told everyone else to 'keep it to yourself.' On the way home one day, when the topic came up, I told Judy that Dad must love her. When she asked why, I told her he would most assuredly beat anyone else about the head and shoulders for touching his cup.

She was upset about her mistake, but I explained that if Dad had been upset with her, she would have known it. "That Dad is laughing at it tells me how much he loves you. It means you are special to him. I wouldn't press your luck and do it again."

It became a standing joke in the family, and Dad told me a few years later that he was beginning to get the bleach taste out of the cup. A smile filled his face as he rinsed it out again.

Just Another Summer Night

There came a night that I will remember for various and obvious reasons until I can no longer do so. It was late August night, closing in on Labor Day weekend, and we had a night off together. I had been telling Judy about the Perseid meteor shower that occurred every year in mid-August. My dad had always taken us out at night to watch them, and it became a lifetime habit.

This particular night, the sky was crystal clear. Even though the peak of the showers had passed, the Earth was not entirely clear of the comet 'Swift-Tuttle', which was responsible for the show. We took a thick blanket to lie out on the grass and lean against the car to watch for streaks of light across the sky.

We were lucky that night. Within two minutes, we had seen several long, bright streaks of light as particles from the comet entered the atmosphere. Judy had seen nothing like she saw that evening, and she ooh and ahh-ed for over half an hour. Eventually, she talked about other things as the light trails diminished, and pretty soon, she began to talk about our relationship.

She told me how she quivered at the sheer happiness of finding me and falling in love. "I suddenly start crying for no reason other than I'm in love with you. It's a wonderful feeling, and now all those love songs I hear on the radio make sense."

In the star-lit sky, I saw her turn to me and wait for my thoughts. "Judy, I can't tell you how you make me feel. I am always thinking about you. I dream about you at night, and no matter what else happens, that you love me keeps me smiling. I have 'loved' others before. But the feelings I have for you aren't even in the same way as those of other girls. It's not even close to what we have together."

We were sitting side by side, me on the right and she to my left, as we began to hug and kiss. No one else was at the house, and the neighborhood was unusually quiet, leaving us with the joy of being close under the beautiful night sky. We had pulled apart for a moment when Judy reached for my right wrist and pulled it toward her. She slipped my hand inside her blouse, placed it on her breast, and leaned into my palm.

While I was temporarily bewildered for a moment, she kissed me again. It's difficult for me to explain my thoughts about what was happening. It was, however, clear to me she knew what she was doing. After a few minutes, she pulled away, and I removed my hand. I started to say something, but Judy cut me off. "I've wanted to do that for a while now. I was hoping you would do it, but I wanted to do it to know how it felt."

She told me she had seen other couples doing such things, and as her confidence in herself and me grew, her curiosity developed as well. Gone, at least for now, were her childhood fears. What I found beside me now were the natural feelings and curiosity of a young lady in love. "Did you like that?" she asked.

I smiled and told her, "I did, very much so. You are a lovely lady, and no normal man could resist you, but I'm not sure we should do this just yet. I don't want you to get hurt again." I started to say more when she once again placed my hand inside her blouse and kissed me again. I was both willing and anxious. While the frightened young lady I had first run into just a year before was gone, I knew well that she could return at any time. I didn't want that to happen.

I didn't know where things would have gone from that night because Steve pulled into the drive just as the intensity built. I wasn't sure which of us was going to be more disappointed. We sat back as if we were going to continue watching the meteor shower, and Judy had just buttoned her blouse when he walked around the car.

"Hey, kids, what ya doing?" I told him we were watching for the Perseids, and he nodded. "Oh, Judy! Lois told me to tell you that you got called in to work the day shift tomorrow." Judy hated day shifts, and she groaned. We stood up and brushed ourselves off. She kissed me and hugged Steve. We watched as she walked to her car and pulled away.

"Don't tell her I said so, but her blouse wasn't buttoned up properly." I knew he was fishing for details, but I wasn't biting. Steve was my best friend, but there were limits to some things. He understood my position on that and knew I would never pry into his relationship with his girl.

As we walked back into the house, he asked me, "You kids are moving right along. I never thought Judy would allow herself to get this close to a guy again, not after that last jerk she went out with two years ago." Steve never knew about her childhood abuse, but he knew that on her last date, the guy was much less than a gentleman with her.

As we got ready for bed, we talked about our relationship. "I've been very cautious with Judy. Do you remember what I told you the first day I saw her?" Steve nodded. "We are getting closer to that eventuality—much closer. Even now, I can barely believe I've found someone like her."

We both went to bed to get rested for the long Labor Day weekend ahead of us. As we drifted off, I knew Steve was thinking about his night with Lois, and I was thinking about my night with Judy. As I fell asleep, I recalled the events of the night. Beyond that, I thought about what my father had told me. I needed to make her mine before someone else had a chance to interfere.

We had been together for just over a year, and I was thinking of asking Judy to marry me. I recalled what the Wicked Witch of the West said in her dying moments in The Wizard of Oz. *'What a world, what a world!'*

Out of Something Horrible

The next few days were horrific ones on the EMS (Emergency Medical System) side of my life. It started with witnessing a murder-suicide, far too up close and personal. The call had begun as a family dispute with injuries. Every cop, medic, and rescue person will tell you that fights among family members are the most dangerous call you can attend.

How this scene was laid out still brings on a case of the shudders many years later. Our unit had to park on a gravel path on the side of a steep hill. I had to walk down to the home at the bottom of a small path that became the house's driveway leading into the house.

As I began my way down the steps, I saw a man striking a woman I later learned was his wife. I had seen a lot of violence in my years, but this guy was seriously intent on hurting the woman. I assumed, remembering how the syllables of that word break down, that as I approached, he would relent, and I'd be left with a screaming match.

That didn't happen.

I was only about ten feet from them when he pushed the woman away from him, leaving me to believe the fight was over. I was wrong.

I took about two more steps closer to the couple, and with no warning, he pulled a pistol from somewhere on his person. He held it out at arm's length and pulled the trigger four times in rapid succession. The sound of the gun paralyzed me as I watched them hit the woman in a tight, circular pattern on her chest.

It was like everything was happening in slow motion. I saw her shirt dimple on the front and puff out on the back. She staggered backward, much like every B-grade movie you may have watched. I heard her grunt as each bullet struck her, and part of me marveled her eyes were wide open during the attack. I didn't notice the blood seep out until just about the moment she fell to the ground.

As I would later tell the law enforcement officers who were just a minute behind me, everything looked like it had been filmed in 'super slow-mo' in my head. As the woman fell to the ground on the right side of my personal movie screen, the man on the left side suddenly pivoted toward me. His weapon was now pointed straight at my chest.

It was and still is difficult for me to measure precisely how long he held that stance. I can still see his eyes giving me an icy stare as his mind contemplated what he would do with me. I vividly recall talking to myself as I realized I had nowhere to run.

I was only five feet from him, and he had nothing to lose if he were to pull the trigger again. The woman that lay to my right was dead, and one more shooting victim wouldn't have mattered one whit if he added me to his list. It seems odd now, but I was not afraid. All I could think was, *I'm too fat to run.*

In the background of this situation, I could hear the sirens of the approaching police units. I also heard my fill-in partner screaming at me to run. I wanted to run, but the rational part of my brain told me to stand still because making a sudden move might cause him to overreact.

It seemed each passing second was more like a minute. In between one of those seconds, our eyes locked. I still have a mental picture of that moment in time, and I knew that the rational part of his mind was shutting down. His pistol was steadily pointed at me for what seemed to be the longest time, but then it quivered ever so slightly. A quick prayer went through my mind. *God? Take care of Judy. Please?*

In the theater of my mind, the slow-motion effect suddenly kicked into hyper-drive. As the man turned almost entirely away from me, he placed the weapon in his mouth and pulled the trigger. In between the time that I heard the round being fired and felt the shower of blood hit me, I saw the police car pull up behind my ambulance.

I can't remember how long I stood there, but his blood was rolling out of my hair and down my face. I remember the first officer on the scene grabbed me and asked if I was alright. His touch broke my paralysis, and my first instinct was to run to the fallen man to see if I could render help.

You might find that odd, but the training always kicked in during times of emergency.

One glance assured me was dead. I ran to the woman lying a few feet away, and although her eyes were still wide open, there was a massive opening in her back. As I knelt beside the woman and her injuries became apparent, the gravity of what had just happened hit me. I remember my partner pulling me back to the rig, checking me out, and washing my face.

I don't remember saying much other than knowing I was lucky to walk away from there alive. My partner kept babbling about what he had seen, but I couldn't tell you a word that he ever said. I was later told that I had given the officers a comprehensive report of the incident. They convinced me to go to the hospital to be checked out.

I tried to tell them I hadn't been hit, but now I know they weren't looking for physical injuries.

I'm not sure of many things from that night, but I'm sure I walked into the Emergency Room under my own power and sat down on a cot. One of the ER docs did what I knew was a neuro-check, and I passed it. The machines they hooked up to me continued with their steady beeping and squeezing.

I remember telling them I was all right and needed to get my ambulance rig ready for the next call. As I said, the training *always* kicked in during emergencies.

Somewhere along the line, someone had told Judy I was in the ER after a shooting. She rushed into the trauma area where they had placed me, expecting me to be injured. Her tears became heavier after seeing that while I was still covered in blood, none of it was mine. I was covered in blood, brains, and skull fragments.

She hugged me tighter than I ever imagined a girl could embrace a guy, and then her training kicked in. She gathered a wash basin of warm water and soap and washed my face and hands clean. I don't remember her words to me, but I remember hearing her voice.

I can only recall a little of the conversation, but I guess I insisted on getting cleaned up and back on the road. The ER doctor wasn't buying that argument, and they got someone, somewhere, to fill in for me for the rest of the night.

One of the police officers took me home and made sure Steve would be there to tend to me. I remember him telling the cop, "This guy will do anything not to work!"

It was how we did business.

I remember Steve helping me get undressed and into the shower. As I allowed the water to run over my head, I saw it turn red then run down the drain. After ten minutes in the bath, I got out and dressed for bed. I finally sat down on the couch, where Steve and I talked for the next few hours. We were more than partners; we were brothers, and he did me more good than anything the hospital staff had done for me.

I don't remember him leading me to my bed, but I slept until about eight in the morning. Just as I was getting up and around, I heard Judy's car pull up, and she entered the house. I could hear Steve talking to her, assuring her I was alright, and that he had been checking on me all night.

I pulled on a ratty old robe and entered the living room, where I was met with another tight hug and multiple kisses. I convinced Judy to allow me to sit beside her, and when we did, she burst out crying. It took a long time to get her to calm down, and I finally convinced her to sleep in my room for the day. I didn't tell her I was going to work with Steve.

I tucked her into bed and kissed her. As I pulled away, she burst out into a series of small sobs. "You could have died! *You could have died!*" Steve knocked on the bedroom door, my warning that he was about to leave for work, and I told him I would be right out.

"Judy, you know our job is a dangerous situation. Any time you deal with people who are upset, angry, or on drugs, there is a chance you can be hurt. The thing you need to keep in mind is that I didn't get hurt. I'm good, really. I'm good." I kissed her forehead and told her to go to sleep and that I would wake her in time to go to work.

The stress had taken its toll on Judy. Within a couple of moments, she was sound asleep. Steve and I slipped out the door, leaving a note on the table that if she needed anything, to call the ambulance base.

During the short drive to work, Steve told me I was crazy for coming back so soon. I told him I might never return if I didn't return just then. He understood what I meant.

In my life as a medic, I was shot twice and stabbed once. This shooting came during a different family dispute, and the other came as a man went through a situation of extreme grief. His parents had been killed in separate car accidents two days apart, and he was devastated. The young man took refuge in a local church and had no intention of hurting me.

I was in the wrong place at the wrong time. He fired the .22 caliber pistol he was holding, and the bullet went through an oak pew and lodged in my right lower calf. The ER doc picked up a set of tweezers and pulled it out.

The stabbing was from a man who was jacked out of his mind on PCP. As often happened with PCP users, they would be very quiet for several minutes, and then they would explode into action. You can call it luck, but I called it 'divine intervention.' Something told me - no, something insisted - that I move my pocket notebook from my right hip pocket and into my left chest pocket.

Less than ten seconds later, the young man exploded forward, pulling a knife from somewhere and hitting me dead center in my chest. The tip of the knife went through the inch-thick notepad and still cut into my left nipple about a half-inch deep. Nearly fifty years later, the scar is still as plain as the day it happened.

I was fortunate, and my only serious injury was during the first shooting. I was shot by a drunk at a bar fight. He was aiming at the guy he had beaten up, but as he pulled the trigger, his level of intoxication caused him to drop the front of the shotgun as he pulled the trigger.

The pellets from the shell hit the frozen pavement, bounced up, and caught me just above the knees and just below my ribs. I spent twelve days in the hospital after that incident, and then I was back at work. I lost my *belly button* and most of my small intestine, but I lived. I could whine about the injury or be thankful that I lived.

Over the next week or so, Judy would have small outbursts over the shooting scene. While my employer wanted to send me to talk to a therapist to 'work out any issues,' I declined their offer.

I had been a medic for several years at that point in my life, and while not usual, violent deaths were a lot more common than you might expect. Suicides, murders, accidents, and other deaths were part of the job. I could settle it in my mind as a case of anger that got out of control.

I was told that Judy had broken down crying at work during a conversation some nurses around her were holding. I saw one of her co-workers during a trip to the ER, and she told me about the situation. I had little time to talk with her then. I knew it boiled down to the fact that Judy had had no one who got close to her and feared losing that support.

On our way to another emergency call, Steve and I talked about it, and I asked him what he thought I should do. He had known her a lot longer than I had, and I knew he would give me real advice.

Many people will provide you with what they think you want to hear. Steve and I were beyond that point, and I expected he would tell me straight.

"Well, my friend, I suspect she needs to hear those four words every woman her age wants to hear." Steve turned the rig into the emergency call driveway, and I shut off the siren. I must have looked at him oddly because, as he got out, I heard him tell me over his shoulder, "Will you marry me? That is the only thing I think that will snap her out of this anxiety thing."

We had gotten used to holding conversations in short bites throughout our partnership. When we had time to ourselves, we could pick up again without missing a beat. As we cleaned the rig up at the hospital, I asked him, "Do you think she would have me? I think we have come a long way in getting her out of her shell. Sometimes, I still worry about her running back down the bunny hole if I act too soon."

With everything cleaned up and ready for our next call, we jumped in the rig and left the hospital "Lois told me the other night that Judy was talking about waiting for you to 'pop the question.' Everyone thought you guys would return married when you went to Vegas."

I told him I had considered that situation, but we hadn't crossed the turning point in our relationship just then. I also told him we had done that now. "Until this shooting deal, Judy had shaken off most of her problems. While this scary event will pass, I know it will be on her mind for a long time. I suppose something else to think about would help."

We backed the ambulance back into the garage and shut the overhead doors when I thought of telling him one more thing. "Say nothing to Lois about this, please? Maybe we can make it a group thing."

Steve smiled and patted me on the back as we returned to the living quarters. "A group thing, huh? What do you have in mind?" We were hanging up our jackets, turning them so we could slip them back on quickly, when the next call came in.

It was only mid-September, but the weather was becoming a bit cooler than average. After three weeks of temps in the high eighties, the sudden onset of highs made me shiver just in the sixties. We spent the rest of the night talking about my plan.

The Setup

It was Steve's turn to cook dinner, and he was busy getting things around. I set the table and then finished the paperwork for the last run we had made. "Well, maybe we could have the girls over here on one of the nights they are off and we are working. I've been thinking about how I might do this proposing thing for a long time now."

The phone rang, and everything came to a stop. While we were getting the first electronic warnings of the time, many of our calls still came in from our dispatch by phone. I grabbed it quickly and was relieved that the hospital was letting us know we had left some equipment there. The ER nurse said they would store it until we rolled in again.

"I thought I would take Judy aside and measure how she is doing, and then if the moment is right, I'll propose and hope she accepts my offer. You never know with these girls. About the time you think you have them figured out, you don't." Steve laughed and agreed with me.

It turned out that I had a lot of time to think before we could orchestrate a night where all of us would be together. Steve and I had to fill in for another medic at another base who had gotten injured on the job. September had left us, and Halloween loomed before everyone would be available.

Steve asked me if I would have a ring to give her, setting off a two-week conversation. While I wanted to be traditional in every way possible, the last thing I wanted to do was have a ring in my pocket and then have Judy say 'no,' or, my bigger fear, have her say 'yes,' and then I give her a ring that she didn't like. As Steve liked to tell me, "Your idea of high fashion is that Pet Rock thing on a necklace you have on your dresser."

I used every trip we took to the big city about an hour away to check out a few jewelry shops. After several stops, I finally found one where I knew one of the guys working in a mall store. I told him what I was looking for and the money I had set aside to spend if she accepted my proposal. The last thing I wanted to happen was to have someone show her a ring that cost five times more than I had to spend.

Steve and I had discussed what I would do that night. There was a small radio station in a town not far away. I got the night guy to agree to play the song I wanted to use for my setup at about ten pm. Planning for every eventuality, I told him that if something had gone awry, I would call him as quickly as possible. These were all pre-email and pre-cell phone days, but I was confident I had everything covered.

It was a Wednesday night, statistically the slowest night of the week, but naturally, we had six calls between four and nine that night. I was about to call the thing off, but it finally broke into the typical Wednesday night silence I was counting on.

Steve and Lois were talking out in the living quarters, and I had managed to secret Judy into our sleeping quarters. We weren't supposed to have visitors in our sleeping area, but this wasn't why the rule was instituted.

Lois did not know what we were going to do. I remember she wanted to watch something on television. I could hear their discussion about watching her show or listening to the radio. I don't know how, but Steve had talked her into listening while they talked on the couch. I knew that was no small miracle itself.

I had spread out a big quilt and sleeping bag on the floor, and we were lying side by side on the edge of the bed, just talking as it got closer to ten pm. I kept hoping each break in his record queue would lead to him playing my song, but he just kept playing other music. About the time I was afraid the DJ had forgotten me, it happened.

"I don't get a chance to do things like this nearly often enough, but I've got a message for a lady named Judy. Someone who loves you very much has a question for you in the form of a song. I hope you will give him the answer he wants to hear."

There was a moment of silence in the air, and then John Denver's voice began to sing 'Follow Me.' I got to my knees and looked up at her. It took her almost five seconds to realize what was happening to her. Her hand went to her mouth, and she began to cry as Mr. Denver implored the lady in his song to 'follow him' in his journeys in life. I looked into her eyes and asked her, "Judy? Would you please marry me?"

Her sobs were getting louder when Lois burst through the bedroom door and saw us. "Girl, you better be telling this guy yes. After all our nights talking about this, you better say yes!" Judy couldn't speak, but she looked at me and nodded her head. Then she hugged me and kissed my face, wetting my uniform shirt with tears.

As I knew would happen, it became that 'group thing' I expected. Before it was over, I think everybody, including Steve, hugged and kissed me. It was one of the happiest days of my life, and I had been able to share it with my best friends.

Everyone was crying and hugging, making my shirt a tear-drenched towel. Nobody cared because they knew I had several spare shirts in the closet.

Heading Down The Aisle

After that night, things flew by at a pace that astounded me. All of Judy's co-workers were almost as excited as she was, and I think a couple of them were even more excited. Word spread faster than a dry season fire, and everywhere I went, someone was congratulating me. I couldn't even fathom how things were going for Judy.

Outside our circle of friends, my dad was the first one we told about what had happened that night. I had always said that I thought Dad loved Judy more than he loved me. It was supposed to have been a joke, but I still think it was true. Dad loved her, and that was all that mattered to me. He smiled more that day than I had seen him smile in years.

This thought was not against my two sisters because our father loved us all. He had taught me early that love was not like a pie, where each slice got smaller as the number of people with whom it was shared grew. Instead, he showed me that the more love you shared, the bigger the pie became.

For reasons I could never explain, I always believed that Dad and Judy were kindred spirits. Both were quiet and loving souls, and I was lucky enough to have them in my life.

It was Judy's family that became the problem. While they accepted me, I don't think they ever seriously thought we would get married. I didn't fit their idea of a husband. Judy's sister had dated several guys working in a local factory. I suppose they always thought that when Judy married, it would be to a factory-working guy.

Everything about me differed from what they had liked about her sister's boyfriends. They graduated from high school and then went to work in the factory. I had gotten a degree at a large and well-known college. I worked as a paramedic in a relatively new field at a time when the local funeral homes ran what passed as ambulances. While her sister's boyfriends had rough hands, mine were soft and smooth. They didn't see how I could support and make their eldest daughter happy.

I suppose it didn't help that we had been officially engaged for nearly a month before she worked up the courage to tell them at a Thanksgiving dinner table. A noisy room went almost stone quiet after she made her announcement. Something in me was laughing, but I suspect that part was laughing to keep the other part of me that was scared, but calm. Her dad and her brothers were big dudes who had worked all their lives in a factory.

I had no problem with her family. I knew I would never fit into the mold that they had in mind. In fact, something that happened because of this situation almost ruined our relationship. Judy's mom visited me at work between Thanksgiving dinner and Christmas. When I saw the look on her face, I knew this wasn't one of those 'Welcome to the family!' visits.

After I directed her to a room where we were relatively alone, she pulled out a massive stack of money and handed it to me. "Take this, please. That is five thousand dollars. Please take it and walk away from my daughter. I don't think you are right for her, and she'll just get hurt. It's better to break this off now rather than a year or so later."

I wasn't sure what to think just then. This was during the early seventies, and five grand was a lot of money. A lot of money!

I stood silently for nearly a minute, trying to gather my thoughts. There was no way I would take her money or not marry her daughter, but I knew my next words would color our relationship for the rest of our lives. Reining in the words I wanted to say, I explained I felt differently. I understood what she told me, but she wasn't the one who should decide what we would do together.

"Over the last eighteen months, I have watched your daughter open up from being a timid and withdrawn girl and become a vibrant and loving woman. Everything about her has changed. She carries herself at work in a completely new manner. She has become confident in her skills and ability to meet and handle new people. I respect you and your family, but I love your daughter more than you ever know or understand."

I watched her face as I handed her the money back and continued. "Please return this money and do something for your family with it. Judy and I are going to get married. We hope it will be with your family's blessing, but with or without it, we are still getting married. I would prefer that you join us in celebrating the start of our lives together, but we are strong enough to do it without you."

I waited for her response, but there wasn't anything to see. Her Mom gathered her things and walked out. I thought I heard her stifle a sob, but I wasn't sure. While I knew she was gone, I knew it wouldn't be the last time I heard about this subject.

I was right.

Before I go much further with this, it needs to be noted for posterity that I understood why this happened. Judy's mom thought she was protecting her daughter. I admire that effort, but her concern was not that I would hurt Judy, but that I wasn't like everyone else they knew. To be honest, I'm not like most people you'd know, but I understood the motive, and I didn't take it personally.

Several days after her mom's visit, Lois called to tell me Judy was in her room and very distraught. She asked me to come over as soon as I could to see what had happened and calm her. I didn't have to 'find out' what had happened because I knew she had visited her parents. I knew precisely what had happened.

I had been doing paperwork for the ambulance service, and as soon as I finished the paper I was working on, I headed to their apartment, roughly fifteen miles away. Visions and nightmares ran through my mind as the miles slipped behind me. While our relationship was strong, I knew it would be long before Judy could take a bump from Life and stay standing upright.

Lois met me at the door and pointed to Judy's room up the stairway. I knocked lightly on her door, and it opened on its own. She lay on her bed, and I could see that she had been crying for a long time. As gently as possible, I sat on the edge of her bed, putting my hand in the middle of her back. "Judy? Tell me, what's wrong? Please?"

It took another five minutes for her to slow down her sobs and gather herself. Gradually, she got to where she could talk to me. "I can't marry you. My Mom says I can't marry you!" She leaned into me and buried her face in my chest. "Why would she do that to me? I just wanted to be happy. Now it's all ruined!" She fell back onto her bed and sobbed into her pillow.

One of the things I had learned long before this event is that some emotions need to play out, or they will only resurface later. It broke my heart to listen to her cries, but I knew that once you reach your rock bottom, it's easier to see that there is a way up to better things. It hurt, but I allowed her to find the bottom of her world as she knew it. I remained at her bedside with my hand on her back.

Eventually, her emotions played out, and she sat beside me again. She started telling me that her mom had forbidden her to marry me and that she needed to break it off as soon as she could. "I'm sorry. I can't marry you."

I reached out and stroked her face, and smiled. "Judy, how old are you?" I knew she was twenty-one but wanted her to tell me that. I heard her whisper her age as she gazed at her feet.

"Alright. You are twenty-one, and the last time I knew, you were old enough to live alone. You bought your car, graduated from one of the toughest nursing schools in the state, and are a respected nurse at your hospital."

Her gaze shifted from her feet to me. Somewhere along the way, we were holding hands. I wasn't sure how that happened or who started it, but it didn't matter. "Listen, dear lady. You are free to do whatever you want to do as long as it is legal. Your Mom can be upset, but she can't stop you from marrying me if that is what you really want to do."

It's been forty-five-plus years since that moment when I saw the girl who fascinated me when we met and became the woman I would love forever. "Listen to me, Judy. Please forgive me for saying this, but your world is exactly that - your world. It will hurt if you don't want to marry me, but I'll understand."

I could see new tears welling in her eyes, but I wanted her to know where she stood. Better yet, I wanted her to understand where we stood. "Judy, you know that if you want to marry me, I'll take you and love you forever. I'll take the things I love about you, and I'll take your shortcomings. I'll take every part of you and smile every day we are together."

I could see her teetering between the girl she had been and the woman the world needed her to be. "You see, those are the rules Dad taught me, and you know how much he loves you. If you will have me, I'm here. I don't care what others think. I've never cared what people think. I only want to know what you think. No one else matters to me anymore. Only you. *Always*, only you. Will you have me?"

It's hard to explain, but for most of my life, I have never seen life as various shades of light and dark. My occupation as a medic demanded that I see things as they were and respond appropriately. Many of my decisions were life and death, and choosing the wrong options could have terrible consequences.

In front of me was the woman with whom I wanted to spend the rest of my life. I was asking her to make a hard decision, probably for the first time in her adult life. I watched her eyes move back and forth, and finally focus on mine as she whispered, "I love you so much; it hurts me. I was afraid you wouldn't want me. I want to marry you and live with you forever." She held me tight and began to cry again, but this time, her tears were from happiness.

Merry Christmas, You May Marry My Daughter!

By the time Christmas rolled around, Judy's mom had walked back from her words several months before and blessed us to be married. I had suspected that would happen. The one thing my father had cautioned me about when I talked to him about what had happened was that I should stay clear of the fight. I had nothing to gain and everything to lose by saying any more than I had told her the day she visited me.

I suppose one of the things that softened the blow was the diamond ring she was wearing. As I had explained earlier, I took her to the jewelry shop where my friend worked, and true to his word; he only brought out items that fell in the price range I had given him. The best memory of that day for me was watching Judy's eyes out-sparkle the diamonds on the display tray.

After talking with Judy briefly, my friend Tim brought out four trays with roughly ten rings per display. He apologized and explained that their security insurance only allowed him to show a certain number of rings at a time.

Tim placed three of the trays in a locked case near us. He smiled as he watched Judy do a little girl jumping on her toes, dancing as he set the first tray of rings out for her inspection.

I pulled up a chair for her near the light by the showing area, and she sat down, still all atwitter. The gentleman showing the rings had taken a few moments to explain what made a diamond valuable, but I doubt she heard many of the tips. She glanced through the first tray and shook her head at all of them, so the man took that tray and brought her the next one with the same result.

At least the third rack of gems held her attention a bit longer, but my nerves began to fray as she shook away the selections. I wondered if I had misjudged her taste, and I think I was tingling as much as Judy had been when the final selections were laid out for her.

I nervously watched as Judy scanned the rings. Her eyes had run along the first line and then back to the bottom set when I saw her stop and zero in on one ring. She asked if she could pick it up, and my friend handed it to her. Her fingers quivered ever so gently as she looked at the diamond from every angle possible. It was the most uncomplicated design on the tray.

She carefully returned it to Tim's hand and turned to me. "May I get this ring? I like it."

I took her hands for a moment. "Dear lady, if you want it, it's yours. You can have any ring on any of those trays. It's your decision." For a moment, I thought she might ask to see the other rings again, but she turned to the man and told him she wanted that ring. Please.

The one thing I did besides setting a price limit was borrow a few pawned silver rings from a friend. He ran a pawnshop down the street from me. I had brought them out on the pretense that I had bought them from a guy hard up for cash, and I wanted to see which ones might fit me.

When none of them fit me, I asked Judy to try them on to see if any of them might fit her. The pawnshop guy had given me six different rings, each a different size. All I had to do was keep the one that fit her the best separate from the rest. Once I had that number, I told Tim her ring size, meaning that every ring she had looked at would have fit her.

Tim put the other rings away, returned them with a pretty little box, and handed them to Judy. Her face went blank for the slightest of moments, and her mouth opened. She looked at me and then at Tim. "Don't you have to size it? Don't we have to pay for it? I'm confused. What should I do?" She returned the box to Tim, who asked her to put the ring on her finger.

Once again, her hands shook as she pulled the shiny gold ring out and watched it slip over her engagement finger. The diamond twinkled in the lights, and that shy little girl smile that I always loved to see slowly emerged. "It fits me perfectly."

Judy slid it off and handed it back to Tim. She whispered to me, "It's beautiful," as Tim walked away with it.

She took my hand and walked back out into the mall. I pulled her back and hugged her. About that time, Tim reappeared with a beautiful box with a bow on it. He handed it to her, along with some papers that told how to keep it clean. She didn't understand, asking if we needed to pay for it.

Tim smiled and said to her, "Your purchase has already been handled. It's all yours. Congratulations!"

There were other things I intended to do in town that day, but Judy was mesmerized by the ring, and I knew nothing else would happen. Once we were in the car, she asked me how I had gotten the ring without paying for it. "Oh, it's paid for already. I told Tim how much I could spend and had him get me the right sizes all set up in advance." Her smile widened.

"Remember playing with those silver rings? I got your ring size from those. I came down here two days ago and wrote him a blank check that he could fill in after you chose. I've known him for several years. It's all yours. Put it on, Sweetie. I want to see it on your finger again."

One might have thought Judy was holding a rare bird in her hands as she opened the box and removed the ring. I asked her to let me look at it for a minute, and she carefully handed it to me. It might have been a simple design, but it fit her persona perfectly. I reached for her hand and gently slid it over her finger.

I saw the tears well and then run down her face as she stared at it. I whispered to her, "I love you, Judy." Then, the stream of tears that had started earlier became a flood. She tried to answer me back, but her voice wouldn't respond. I told her it didn't matter; I knew what she wanted to say. I could see her look at the ring and then at me all the way home.

I tried not to get all goofy, but my eyes betrayed me. My heart was singing as the impact of what had just happened. We were going to get married!

The Countdown Begins

I had given Judy full control of all the wedding plans and when it would happen. I told her I only wanted a week's notice to be sure I could get my suit cleaned and time off for the honeymoon. It wasn't until Christmas dinner at her parent's house that I was told we were getting married in early March of the next year, a mere seventy days away. I guess the girl was in a hurry.

Judy and her friends made all their plans at work, and then every few days, I'd be updated on what was happening. They traveled to a store on the south side of a nearby major city that carried all kinds of wedding dresses for the bride and her court. I got a call asking me what color my suit would be. I no more than told her it would be black when they hung up amidst a lot of giggling.

Many girls like to set their wedding day a year or more down the road. When Judy set hers for less than three months, I must have been asked a dozen times or more if she was pregnant. I responded indignantly, *'How dare you ask me that, and it's none of your business! After all, you don't need to worry about the consequences if you aren't taking the chances.'*

Every time Lois and Judy visited us at the ambulance base station, it was nothing short of a giggle-fest. I found it refreshing to hear Judy laughing, but Steve and I always joked about the maturity level we were seeing. It made for a happy New Year's attitude for all of us.

Lois cornered me one day and wanted to know our honeymoon plans. Hoping to get a rise out of her, I asked her what she had in mind. She playfully slapped me and asked me again, telling me she wanted to know what kind of clothing Judy would need to bring. I had a smart response, but I kept it to myself just then.

With a straight face, I told her, "My plans right now will take us to Florida, near the new Disney World location that opened just a few years ago. We went to Disneyland when we were in California, and I thought it would be nice to go to Disney World."

When we first met, I told Judy I was like Peter Pan, the eternal little boy, and wanted to visit the new Disney park. Years into our marriage, I had to remind her several times that I had warned her.

Lois kept asking me questions; naturally, she wanted to know where we might be staying. I guess it was a maid of honor thing. "I did some calling around and found a nice Hyatt Hotel just five miles away in a town named Kissimmee. From there, it would be about ninety minutes to either coast, and we can walk in the Atlantic and the Gulf just like we walked in the Pacific. Very few people have ever walked in all three bodies of water."

There were other questions, and I eventually answered them to her satisfaction. I know Judy was extremely close to Lois, and talking to one was the same as talking to the other. In an odd quirk of fate, Lois and Steve were married in July, four months after we were married. He was my best man, and we just swapped roles four months later.

A Near Disaster

Everything seemed to fall right into place, with the wedding less than ten days away. We had met with my former pastor, who had been a good friend to me for years. About six months before our marriage, he had been moved as a minister to a new church. When I called him, he told me he would consider it an honor to travel back to his old ministry to marry us.

We met with him and talked for almost two hours. The pastor and his wife found Judy the exact type of woman they thought I would ultimately find and marry, which made me happy.

Steve and I had our suits, as did Judy's brother and my two brothers I had asked to be in our ceremony. Judy and Lois had their dresses on order and had set her sister up with a beautiful dress as well. One of the girls from the hospital completed the marriage court, and all was good. That was until the telephone rang four days before our wedding date.

The lady on the other end asked for Judy, who happened to be there at the time. I handed the receiver to her and went to do something else outside. When I came back, everything had turned upside down in a matter of two minutes. Judy was in my room, crying her eyes out, with Lois trying to comfort her.

When I asked Steve what had gone wrong, he told me that an accident at the bridal shop had destroyed Judy's dress. Even worse, getting a new one tailored for her would take at least three weeks. I didn't need that headache just then, but I knew I had to fix it for her.

I called the bridal place back and asked if there was anything they could do to help me with this problem. Fortunately, I was talking to one of the younger ladies who worked there who understood my nightmare.

She explained that if I wanted to go elsewhere, she would arrange an immediate refund of the seven hundred dollar dress that Judy had picked out. I told her it would be nice, but it was Tuesday, and we were scheduled to marry on Saturday. I heard a perceptible change in her voice and a brief silence as she went to another room to avoid being overheard.

"Sir, I understand the problem. Don't tell anyone I told you this, but there is a bridal shop that just closed down, and we have been buying a lot of their inventory. If you call down there and tell them that Julie sent you, they will sell her a new dress at a discounted price at their cost." I took the number and the address and thanked her profusely.

I made my way to where the girls were crying and explained to Lois what I had found out. I knew Judy was devastated and would need the support only Lois could provide at that moment. As she headed to the phone to call the new bridal shop, I sat beside Judy. It took several minutes to convince her to at least make the trip to look at their inventory.

She was entirely convinced that everything was going to be ruined, and there was no sense in wasting more time. I told her to get up and get moving, or I'd be forced to marry her in her underwear. She sobbed out a laugh and went to the bathroom to wash her swollen face.

When she stepped out, Lois explained she had talked to the woman at the closed-up store. The woman had told her that if they got down there before the end of the day, they would custom-fit it for her while they waited.

The girls gathered their things, and before they left, I slid up to Steve and asked him if he could float me seventy-five bucks. I had a single one-hundred-dollar bill in my pocket. I figured that rather than waste the time of them going to get the refund, they could at least seal any deal they might secure at the new place. He pulled out his wallet and handed me another hundred dollars, which I gave to Lois. Judy was still upset, and I didn't trust her to hold on to the money in her current state.

As I remember, it was about ten in the morning when the girls left. Steve and I were called out to back up our unit in a massive accident about three miles from our house, making it easier to wait for their return. I did some paperwork, and Steve ran back to the master medical base to get the supplies we needed after running day and night the last couple of days.

With no word of what was happening, we made a late lunch. It was about four in the afternoon. I think Steve had just eaten his sandwich when we heard a car in our driveway. Unsure of what we would find, we stepped onto the porch to see two young ladies with big smiles.

I was just about to ask what had happened when Judy gave me a big hug that lasted a minute or more. Lois explained the day and the people they had met. It turns out that Julie, the girl who had told me about their store, had called them and explained the situation. They met them at the door, locked it behind them, and asked what Judy was looking to wear.

I've never been a fashion nut, so none of the terms they were using made sense to me, and I asked that she just 'cut to the chase.' Lois gave me a wrinkled face that inferred I should be quiet and listen. "It turns out that they had a dress that was virtually identical to the one Judy had ordered from the other place. It was the same color and was only missing one piece of a veil, and they found one that would match the dress for her."

I almost asked what shade of white might have matched the dress, but seeing that everyone was smiling, I figured I would just be quiet. Lois continued to explain that this dress only needed to be adjusted in two small places to make it fit her as if it had been tailored for Judy. Steve and I were nodding our heads along with her words as her story wound down when Judy jumped in.

"The best part." Judy's voice failed her a moment. "The very best part of all of this came when we asked how much it was going to cost us." Again, her voice choked up. "They gave it to me! The lady said they felt so bad about the other dress being destroyed and that they could see I was so upset that they just gave it to me! Isn't that wonderful! The dress is in the back of the car, and everything is perfect again."

A lot of hugging, kissing, and crying followed the story, and I think it would be safe to tell you that the girls weren't the only ones who cried. I remember whispering to Judy during a particularly long hug, "I told you, dear lady, this marriage is destined to be." She started crying again and held me even tighter.

Almost There

The next few days went by like a whirlwind, even for a laid-back guy like me. To help get a few extra days off for our honeymoon, I worked as many days as I could fit in. The girls had scheduled a wedding rehearsal on the Friday afternoon before we were actually to get married. I was working, and as I knew it would happen, we had a last-minute transfer from one hospital to another, and we had to make it a Friday evening situation.

I had never attended a wedding rehearsal before and thought everything had gone fine. It was quickly explained to me I was so desperately wrong. According to some lady whom I never figured out who she was or why she was there, short of making a spectacle of herself, everyone had made 'major mistakes.' I got caught whispering to Steve that inviting this woman was the only 'major mistake' I saw.

Everyone but the lady to whom I was referring thought it was funny.

I was dead tired from the schedule I had been keeping and the number of emergencies I had handled in the last three days. All I wanted to do was to go home and rest. I found out that wasn't in the cards, as I had to stay there for the rehearsal dinner and some social hours.

I wanted to spend time with Judy, at least, but she was surrounded by an endless sea of friends and co-workers. It was plain to see that she was enjoying her time in the sun, and I wasn't going to spoil that for her.

Even Steve was tied up talking to various people in attendance, so I found a corner chair at the table and waited for people to find me. Judy's grandmother on her dad's side found me, sat beside me, and held my hand. "You look tired, dear, but these girls are having a good time. Judy will remember this night for all of her life." I nodded my understanding and was about to say something else when she stopped me.

"I know there was some talk that you might not be the right man for Judy, but I want you to know something. From the first time I saw the two of you together, it was clear that you brought something in her to life. Judy has always been a hard worker, but was never a social butterfly like her sister."

Now and then, someone stopped by my little corner and congratulated me on our happiness. I shook their hand and thanked them. Just as fast as they had stopped, they were gone.

Grandma B smiled as they left and then continued. "I am so happy that she has found someone who cares for her the way you do. I've seen her eyes light up when you touch and hold her hand. I'm an old lady, but I know genuine love when I see it. If you treat each other nicely, your life will be filled with love forever. Few folks find 'forever love.' I think you have it with Judy."

My oldest brother stopped by to tell me he was leaving, and I thanked him and hugged him. I looked up and saw that things were winding down, and others were preparing to go. I said something to Grandma B that I should at least say goodbye to some of these people, and I stood up. She wasn't very tall, but she stood, and pulled me down to hug her.

During the hug, she whispered to me, "I spoke with your daddy, and I can tell that he taught you well. Take care of my Judy. She loves you in a way most will never understand. Treat her well, and she will be the best thing that ever happened to you." I promised her that her granddaughter would be the center of my life from here on out, and we parted.

I was still bone-tired, but I felt much better after our talk. I spent the next fifteen minutes thanking people I didn't know for showing up. When the hall was almost empty, Steve found me and hugged me. "You are one lucky son of a gun. You know that, don't you?" I did indeed know that, and we headed to the parking lot, our arms around each other.

The trip home was uneventful, and I fell asleep for the last time as a single man. You've all heard the phrase, *Attitude is everything*. I've known that to be true for most of my life. I've learned, that in particularly trying times, it is not only your attitude but your expectations, too.

Just then, I had some high expectations.

Along the path of our lives, many things were to go horribly wrong, but we always found that together, we would come out of an event only slightly less for wear. Having witnessed how people lived and died during my career as a medic and then as an ER nurse, I learned that an expectation of your outcome is just as important as your attitude, maybe even more critical. My last thought as I drifted off was that from here on out, I expected to be happy forever after.

From This Day Forward

Everything considered, I slept very well that night. I didn't even set my alarm, and after about nine hours of deep sleep, I awoke feeling great about 8:45 the next morning. I stopped at the ambulance base and made sure everyone was set for my extended vacation. One of the crew reminded me I needed to sign a couple of papers that needed to go into the home office next week. I thanked everyone there, shook everyone's hand, and was gone.

Steve and I met at a local trucker diner and ate our last breakfast as roommates. We had lived together for five years, and it was difficult to realize we wouldn't be doing that anymore. He and Lois had just officially announced they were going to get married in four short months behind us, so we told everyone we were swapping roomies.

When we were finished, I went to visit my dad. As the oldest of six kids, I was able to spend a lot more 'one-on-one' time with him as a boy. The rest of the kids spent more time with him than I did, but I got to have more time *alone* with him. We worked the farm together from the time I was six until he sold it when I was about sixteen.

For a lot of other reasons, I left home just before I was sixteen. Things at home were changing, and the way people lived life itself was changing with the times. I know you've heard it a hundred times, but life was simpler back then. It sounds cliché, but my life before I was sixteen changed significantly when I became seventeen, and it had nothing to do with leaving home.

Everything just changed.

I pulled into Dad's drive, went into his big antique round oak table, and sat down. He got up to get me a cup of coffee and asked if I wanted it ruined. That was Dad's way of asking if I wanted cream and sugar. He knew I did, but it was one of those long-running jokes we were lucky enough to enjoy.

As I think about it now, I realize Dad was a good man and an even rarer father figure, and I would have never accomplished a tenth of what I have done in life without him. Man, I'd be kidding if I didn't tell you how much I missed him now.

As I was writing those last couple of paragraphs, it was like being slapped in the face. I know he would be able to tell me how to stop feeling the way I do right now. My college and my job would keep me far away from him for most of the next twenty years before he died.

I was supposed to have been with him about the time he died at home, but I had been held up doing something for someone else. As a medic and then a nurse, I can tell myself that there would have been not one darn thing I could have done to stop his death. I knew that, but at least I would have been there. It still eats at my mind some thirty years later.

You didn't see it, but I just had to wipe my eyes and face. *Again.* We never expect those things. Do you know what I mean?

We sat around the table, just Dad and me, drinking coffee, telling tales from the long-ago past, and laughing about them. When I finally asked him for advice on this day, he stopped talking and stared out the window at the pond between the house and the road for several minutes. I could never recall seeing him think so long about answering a question for me.

I heard him sniffling, kind of like I was as I wrote this passage, before he took a deep breath. "Boy, you've already got half the battle won with that girl you're going to marry. A man could go another lifetime and not find such a woman. Remember how lucky you are every single day of your life. Don't argue with her because the silly fights will always lead to trouble with your woman."

Dad had emptied his coffee cup, and stood to fill it again. He made a gesture to ask if I wanted more, but I declined. He sat back down, took another deep breath, and sighed.

"If you put Judy before yourself, you're going to do just fine. If there comes a day that she wants something enough that she wants to argue with you, I can tell you right now that you will be wrong. Just tell her, 'Yes, dear,' and let her have her way. You'll be so much happier in life if you do."

"It doesn't take a genius to see that there's not a mean bone in her. She will love and respect you if you only do the same." Dad's face went blank for a few minutes as he sipped his coffee. I couldn't help but think that he recalled events that had led to his divorce just a couple of years before. I was probably the only one of the kids who saw what was happening.

My mom had an emotional issue. No matter what Dad had tried to do for her, it was never enough, and it would never have been enough. She wasn't the girl he had married after she had been kicked in the head by a cow.

Nothing serious, but I can remember how she changed and how they drifted apart. I was angry about it as it happened, but I learned to put the anger away as I eventually came to grips with her illness.

I could see that those memories were running through his mind, and I felt terrible about stirring those thoughts up on this particular day. I started to say something to that effect, but he stopped me. "Learn from that situation, son. I could have changed a few things. I don't know if those things would have changed anything, and maybe I didn't put enough effort into it. Learn from my mistakes."

Dad took in another deep breath and looked up at the old 'Master Mix' feed store clock he had on the wall. It was getting on in time to head toward the church. "I'm just telling you not to get headstrong with this girl. It may take you ten, maybe even twenty years, but someday, you'll wake up and think about this day, and you will thank God for giving this girl to you. Don't you ever hurt her. Don't raise your hand to her. I didn't raise you that way, and I better never hear that you did something like that because you'll never be too big to get a whipping."

Once again, I'm wiping my face.

I can remember those words Dad gave me almost verbatim. He was an everyday man in his words and his deeds. I knew if I came to him and asked him for advice, he would give me wisdom for the rest of my life. I followed his words as best I could, and when I had time to talk with my son several decades later, I told him those same words.

Finally, I knew I had to get to the church and get ready. The times I had with Dad were getting further apart, and we both knew it. We had just spent about half an hour, only the two of us. Other than riding in a vehicle together a few years later, I never had that much time with him again. I got to spend longer times with him, but never again one on one.

It is something I will regret forever.

Finally!

I thanked Dad for his time and put my hand out to shake his, but he wasn't having that. He pulled me in and hugged me for nearly a minute. I think we both understood that our relationship would change after this day. I asked him when he was going to head up. He drank the last bit of his coffee and said he just had to shower and get his suit on, and then he would be right behind me.

This time, Dad stuck his hand out, and we shook hands. All of those years as a farmer had given him a firm grip. For one last moment, I was a boy again.

Dreams of walking out in the pastures, working on the electric fence that kept the cattle in their field. I dreamed of going swimming in the pond after the day was over, or laying out on the grass to watch the stars in the summer nights.

The scenes from my childhood went by in fleeting memories—watching him put up bales of hay, tossing the heavy bales around like they were empty boxes. I realized how hard he had worked all of his life, and he never complained about anything. As I would say at his funeral, there never would be a way I could escape his shadow, but I never wanted to do so.

It's hard to outrun your childhood memories. I never wanted to forget them. I was ten miles down the road before my eyes cleared up.

It was March in Michigan, and naturally, a light snow began to fall. I had just had my Monte Carlo serviced and replaced the tires, making it easy to hold the road. I remember little of the trip, but soon, I found myself pulling into the church's parking lot.

Steve met me there and took my keys. "I was told not to give you a way to escape!" We laughed and hugged, and as I walked into the church with my clothes in a plastic bag, I told him not to put too many cans on the back of it. He giggled and walked away.

Things were jumping inside the place. The moment I was inside, someone grabbed me and hustled me into a side room, told me to get changed, and then just stood there. I didn't have a clue who the woman was. I was about to ask her if she was going to help me dress when she finally walked out.

I took a deep breath and changed my clothing. I could hear the bustling outside my dressing room, and I said a little *'thank you'* for my momentary bit of silence. I was looking at my tie in the mirror when the mystery woman came back in and looked me over.

She turned my collar down, squared my tie, and then hauled me into another room. I found the photographer waiting to take several shots of me standing there. He took me out into the church's main room so he could take photos of me and the various windows and candles.

In between him loading more film into the camera, someone told me they had already taken pictures of Judy. When I asked how she had looked and how she was holding up, the photographer turned to me and smiled.

"Judy was absolutely radiant. She has a beautiful smile. I could see that she was nervous but doing just fine." To be honest, I was rather amazed by that news. Judy had been a bundle of nerves the last time we had been together. I was soon to learn that when she turned her mind to the task at hand, there was no one better. "You're a lucky man, Mr. Greenhoe. A fortunate man."

I thanked him, but I already knew just how lucky I was.

I looked at the clock and saw that there was just shy of an hour left before the start of the wedding. I stood out in the foyer and greeted a lot of people I had never seen before today.

I was pretty good with names, but couldn't have recalled a single one three minutes later. I saw Dad in the room where they had taken my pictures. I talked to him for a minute, and someone asked me if my mother was going to be there, and I told them I didn't know.

I never knew who made the call, but they pulled in one of my favorite aunts to pose with Dad. Aunt Phyllis looked beautiful, standing there with Dad, and I still have that photo near my writing desk. Dad had a big smile, and I could see he was happy for me.

As it turned out, my mom never showed up. Many years later, she apologized. I had learned that it was best to accept the apology and smile. As Dad always told me, things happen, and time passes, and you can't do a darn thing about things already gone by you.

I had been lucky twice. I had been raised by a man who spent a lot of time with me, and I was marrying a woman who would do the same. I think the right word is *blessed.*

I think I was talking to a man I didn't know when my entire crew from the ambulance base showed up. They had gotten coverage from another station and came up to watch me be *'led into a harness.'*

It was good to see familiar faces in a sea of strangers. Judy's dad was an executive for a big company, and he had invited a ton of people. To be honest, I didn't care who else was there as long as Judy was there.

I barely had time to thank my crew when that same pushing woman told me it was time to get toward the front of the church. I spent a moment talking with some of Judy's family, who had made it to their seats in the front couple of rows. When I saw Grandma B, I had to squeeze down the aisle, hug her, and whisper, 'Thank you.'

I was getting a whispered yell, telling me to get back where I was supposed to be. I leaned over to Steve, my best man, and told him, "Remind me to slip that woman some rum so she can't gripe all the time." We both giggled, and I got the 'look' again. I didn't care because I would never see that woman again.

Steve and I were talking quietly when the people behind us suddenly went dead silent. Just as I turned around, the organ lady began to play the traditional wedding march, and I smiled and kicked into *'marry mode.'*

With their baskets of flower petals, the young girls came down the aisle and took their places to the left. The rest of the various ladies of the wedding court made their way toward us, all in a locked-step march.

I smiled at each of the girls as they approached and then broke to the left. The aisle cleared for a moment, and the music stopped, leaving me eager to see my girl come forward. When the organ began again, signaling that the bride was on her way, my heart swelled as I first saw her clear the entryway.

Judy was heading toward the altar, her dad holding her arm. His huge smile told me he was extremely proud of his daughter.

As Judy grew closer, I saw that shy smile that had caught my eye so long ago break across her face. Our eyes locked, and at that very moment, our hearts locked.

They did the traditional, "Who gives this woman to be married to this man?" Everyone could hear the pride in her dad as he spoke his words, "Her Mother and I."

He stepped aside and gave me her arm, and I felt Judy move her hand down my arm and then squeeze my hand.

People who know me will tell you that there have been precious few times that I was speechless, but just at that exact moment, I couldn't speak. Judy's face was a beacon from heaven to me, and the love I felt right then overwhelmed me. I was doing my best not to cry, but her smile saved me.

We stood before over one hundred people and pledged ourselves to each other. I promised her that there would never be a time that I would leave her. No matter where I was, I'd be there whenever she called. I told her that her love would be all that I would ever need from this moment on until we were no more. Her voice was hesitant at first, but she read her vows back to me, pledging that she would stay with me no matter what befell us.

My minister friend spoke for a moment about how long he had known me and that he had fallen in love with Judy when he had met her. He explained to our families and friends that he just knew that our coupling would be forever.

After a brief prayer, he called to the ring bearers to come forward. Lois took my ring from the little girl, and as she stepped away, I saw a big, toothy smile. I smiled back at her, and she blushed.

I kept my gaze on Judy, but I could see Steve take the ring he had brought on a red velvet pillow out of the corner of my eye. The little boy flashed me a big smile and showed me the cushion to prove that he hadn't dropped it as he had in practice the night before. I heard Steve whisper, 'Good job!' to him as he turned to retake his place, waving at me as he went back.

The minister had us face each other, and to be honest, I can't remember if I made my vows first or if Judy did. I remember the words like they were yesterday. "*I, Verwayne, take you, Judy, to be my lawfully wedded wife, to have and to hold from this day forward, for better or for worse, for richer, for poorer, in sickness and in health, to love and to cherish; from this day forward until death do us part.*"

I remember that as Judy made the same vow, her voice was ever so soft. Her eyes were locked on mine, and she told me later that she only wanted me to hear them. It didn't matter to me. I had heard them, and so did the good reverend.

The minister made his speech about being faithful and tender with one another. There were other words spoken, but all I saw was my Judy standing there, her eyes welling with tears and her smile growing bigger.

Finally, we got to the best part. *"By the power vested in me by God and the state of Michigan, I now pronounce you husband and wife. You may kiss your bride."* It's a lot more common now than it was back then, but as we kissed for about ten seconds or more, I heard the clapping and cheering as it went up from the pews.

I had completely forgotten that there were other people in the church at that moment. The only thing I knew was that I was holding my wife.

My wife!

We turned as we had practiced the night before, and then I heard the words I wanted to hear. *"Ladies and gentlemen, I give you, Mr. and Mrs. Verwayne and Judy Greenhoe!"* I've been to baseball games that didn't get the roar that I heard that day. Somewhere in the background, I heard the organ lady begin the exit music, and we turned to leave.

Judy had a tight grip on my arm, and it was all I could do to keep her from running down the aisle. She told me later she just wanted to get away from everyone and be alone.

Everything became a dream sequence as we finally cleared the main entrance and then took a position in a greeting line that seemed to go on forever. I spoke with so many people for a good twenty minutes for brief moments, and I knew I'd never remember them all.

About the time everyone had cleared, the photographer reassembled the wedding party for photos at the front of the church. I knew it was tradition, and we would cherish these photos as our lives went by, but I just wanted to talk to my wife right then.

I had lost track of time, but finally, the pushy lady told me we had roughly twenty minutes to make it to where they were holding the reception. I had never been inside the place, but I knew where it was, and I knew we would have time to slip away and talk.

As it turned out, as I was making my way to the dressing room, I saw that one of the bathrooms was open. I grabbed Judy, pulled her in with me, and locked the door. Finally, alone, we took a moment to hold each other with no one watching, no one interrupting, and no pushy woman telling me where I had to be.

We were alone with each other, and suddenly, it seemed enough just to be alone.

We stood there for about five minutes, occasionally kissing and softly exchanging our three-word promise. '*I love you.*' I don't know how to explain to a person who has never married or someone who married without the love we shared, but our kisses were different. Judy's touch on my face was different.

We were different, and it was beautiful.

Of Toasts and Dances

As we got into Steve's car and headed toward the reception, the snow began to fall a little faster, giving me hope we would be home that evening at a decent hour. Our honeymoon plans were to leave home at about nine in the morning to be in Kissimmee, Florida, at about noon the next day.

I severely misjudged the crowd.

We arrived at the reception to find a massive line of revelers waiting outside in the snow. As I went inside, I told Judy, "The party isn't going well until the first drunk passes out!" Neither of us was a drinker, but we were in the minority on that subject.

It only took about a minute for the pushy lady to find us, herd us to the head table, and then yell for everyone to take a seat. I looked down at the champagne glasses in front of us and was about to say something when Steve whispered to me, "Don't worry, you two are getting Vernor's Ginger-Ale, ya sissy!"

We both went into a small giggling spell, which drew a sharp rebuke from the pushy lady. I stopped for a second and whispered to Steve, "Who is this woman?" sending us both into another giggling fit. I didn't care because I knew I could walk out anytime, and I wanted to leave in about thirty minutes.

Despite our boyish games, the reception group quieted and looked up at us. Someone began the goofy tradition of spoons clanging on glasses and chanting, *"Kiss, kiss, kiss!"* I had no problem with that, but Judy was shy. It took a lot more clanging to convince her it would not stop until she stood up and kissed me. An enormous cheer went up, allowing Judy to sit back down, leaving me standing there.

I was about to say something when the clanging started again, this time demanding a *"Speech! Speech!"* Having spent a few thousand hours teaching CPR and First Aid classes, speaking to large groups was an old-hat thing to me. I held my hand up and waited for everyone to quiet down again.

Once the noise level fell to an acceptable level, I began the speech I had written out a few days before. "On behalf of my better half, I want to thank you all for being here tonight, especially with all that snow coming down. It means so much to us to be able to celebrate our love with you. I promised Judy I would keep this short, so allow me to make a toast."

I smiled as I saw hands across the room reach for their drinks. When everyone was holding their glasses up, I handed a glass to Judy and asked her to stand up with me. "Folks, I am so honored to stand here tonight with my lovely bride, and I want to promise you she will always be the love of my life. Her needs will come before mine, and there will never come a time when that will change."

A big applause ovation broke out, started by the rowdies of my ambulance crew. I waited for the crowd to settle down again and finished my toast. "Here's to my wife. Isn't that a lovely thing to say? *My wife!* I can barely believe it myself. Here's to my wife, I will love you forever. For our families, here is to you. We are all one big family now, and I can only imagine the nightmares that will give some of you! Thank you for being here!"

Glasses were hoisted, shouts of approval were made, and I kissed my wife again.

We were led over to the table where the cake had been placed. Judy's friends were urging her to smear my face with cake, but she was too much of a lady to do that. We each had a small piece of the cake, and our exchange was a clean and happy affair. The photographer had missed the shot, and we had to restage it again. It was an exceptionally good cake, so I didn't mind.

One last time, the pushy lady pulled me aside and told me that Judy and I had to go to a specific table and wait for the first dance. I gave the DJ a particular song I wanted him to play. It never occurred to me that my co-workers, led by a *brother from another mother*, would sabotage me. I don't know why I didn't think about it, but I knew exactly who was to blame when it happened.

It took the DJ a few minutes longer to move things around than the pushy lady had thought. She kept telling me we had to stand there and be ready to go when the DJ started talking. Judy and I were talking about our trip to Florida when we heard his mic kick on with a loud click.

His patter was perfect right up until I heard him tell everyone that friends of the groom had given him his favorite song and to quote them, not the 'sissy song' his new wife wanted me to play. So here it is, Verwayne's favorite song, "Your Cheatin' Heart!"

The lights dimmed down to a small circle in the center of the room. Judy was giggling hysterically because she knew I hated that song. She knew I was mad, but she whispered to me, "It's a joke, dear. Please dance with me?"

Out of the love of my new wife, I calmed down, showed my fist to my 'buddies,' and led Judy to the center floor, where we danced. About halfway through the song, Steve and Lois joined us. As they got close enough, I told Steve that he would never be safe until this act of sedition was avenged. This set everyone in our little dance group into a giggle storm.

You never know the depth of friendship until you are in love. Steve told me he would make it right, and they danced over to the rest of the ambulance crew and sent them to the DJ with new instructions.

My 'special song' finally ended, and the DJ broke in again. "Folks, I was just told that I was an unwitting participant in a prank. I didn't know that, and I apologize to our newlyweds. Please allow me to play the originally requested song for them. I'm sorry. I'm sure the newlyweds wouldn't mind if you joined them after a minute of dancing solo to their actual song."

I gave a salute to the guy and waited. The speakers began to play the song I had chosen, "You" by the Carpenters. As Karen's sweet, rich voice told her story, Judy and I danced for what I had wanted the first time. I will confess that I was the first one to cry as the music played.

While the DJ had told the crowd that they could join us mid-song, we danced alone through the entire song, and to be honest, that was just fine with me.

The rest of the night went by like a dream. There were dances and the opening of gifts, plus a steady flow of people who wanted to wish us the best. Every so often, I would be given an envelope, and most would tell me it would help us have a better honeymoon and get on our feet. It wasn't until the next morning that I realized we had collected over seven thousand dollars.

Around eleven at night, the party was still going strong, but both Judy and I were beyond tired. I grabbed Steve and asked him to tell everyone we were leaving. The last thing I wanted to do was get on the far side of the room and get tied up in a conversation with someone I didn't know. I looked around the room and couldn't seem to locate the pushy lady, and I asked Judy to say goodnight to her family.

A few minutes later, the friends who knew us best were gathered by the exit, giving us all hugs and handshakes. We stepped outside into the cold and found three new inches of snow. One of the guys from the ambulance crew took my keys and told me he would bring them around to the front entrance.

We took one last opportunity to say goodbye to Steve and Lois and wished them luck as they moved in together. I hugged Lois as Steve embraced Judy. Lois told me, "You take care of that girl. I mean it. Take care of her, or I'll come to kick you silly in the middle of the night!" The scary part of that threat was that I knew she could and would do it. I promised her that all would be well.

I laughed as I heard the Monte Carlo come around the corner with about twenty cans and shoes dragging behind it. Someone got a photo of Judy and me standing behind it, a shoe in my hand and a confused look on my face. One of the guys removed them and put them in his trunk, promising to give them to us when we returned.

A few more people strayed out to watch us leave. As emotional as all that was, I was glad to be alone in the car with Judy. We had a forty-five-minute drive to get back to our home without the snow, but we ended up making the trip in just under an hour. It was pretty slippery on our doorstep, but I managed to carry her inside and gently put her back on her feet.

I guess it was the sudden reality that we were married and could do anything we wanted. We both knew what everyone thought we might do, but we were tired of a long trip ahead of us the next day. I held my wife close to me and whispered, with a slight leer in my voice, "Do you know what I want to do?"

I saw her smile, and she nodded. "You got it, dear; let's go to bed and get some sleep!"

It was a crazy night after a very long day. I had taken off my suit and hung it in the closet. Judy had been instructed how to store her wedding dress, and I observed her fold it and place it back in its box. It was cold outside, but our home was nice and warm.

We took our showers and met in the living room, Judy in her nightgown and me in an old bathrobe. Somehow, my bed had been covered with gifts that someone with a key had dropped off, and I was too tired to move them. Judy pointed to the extra mattress that had been tossed on the floor after Steve had moved his things out. "Works for me, my lady! Shall we?"

I grabbed a pile of blankets that had been tossed on one of the living room chairs, and a minute later, we lay snuggled beside each other. We were holding hands and stealing kisses from each other, and we whispered to each other for a few minutes about the events of the day.

Without even realizing it, we fell asleep in each other's arms. My last thought of the night had been, 'I bet no one envisioned us doing this tonight!' Until now, we told no one that we just went to sleep that night.

We were in love, married, and happy. Life lay ahead of us.

Heading South

The next morning, we awakened almost at precisely the same time. The weather had warmed during the night, and some of the snow was melting away. We made some coffee, and I loaded our luggage into the car while Judy showered. When she was out, I took a shower while she made sure that I had gotten everything she thought we would need. We checked the furnace and all the oven knobs. As a bonus, I threw the electric box switches to ensure there wasn't much of anything running.

We talked for a minute about going to one of the local restaurants but decided against it. We just wanted to get on the road and get warm. Although we had driven across the country before, this felt different. Judy seemed more confident in herself and wanted to hold hands while we traveled.

I was on the Interstate, southbound, in less than an hour, and we were out of Michigan in less than three hours.

It's amazing how fast a 1,400-mile trip can go when you are goofy in love. State after state melted behind us, and soon we were in the mountains of Kentucky and Tennessee. We hit Georgia at about seven pm, and I pulled off at a rest area to grab a nap.

Judy wondered why we didn't keep on moving. "If you are too tired, I can drive!" She had never been through Atlanta, but I had. I explained about the high level of traffic at this time of the night, telling her that if we could wait an hour, most of it would drop off.

I don't think I got much rest because we had so much to discuss related to our trip. Judy wanted to lay out our future, talking about where we could move my bed. She wondered if her bigger bed would go into what would be our bedroom. I assured her that if it could be made to fit, my crew would make it go.

I must have drifted off somewhere along the line, and I awoke to Judy getting back into the car. I looked at my watch and made my trip to use the rest area facilities, and we were back on the freeway in a matter of minutes. We hit the outskirts of Atlanta, and I knew I could use the bypass routes or go straight through. I stayed the course, and while the traffic was still much heavier than I wanted to be in just then, I knew we would glide on through with virtually no slowdowns.

As soon as the traffic thinned some, Judy was fast asleep. I kicked on the cruise control and kept on driving. It was a beautiful night in southern Georgia, and I had much to ponder. A new wife meant a new lifestyle for me. Before Judy, my life had been spent in college dorms and sharing a place with other guys. I never realized how much my life was about to change.

By the middle of the state, it became a downhill ride, and the car's engine slowed without ever dropping any speed. The nighttime traffic was smooth, and I just stayed between the semi-trucks, and we maintained a steady 73 mph.

As the sun began to break the eastern sky, we crossed over the Georgia state line into Florida. I knew there was a beautiful rest area about twenty miles in, and about the time I pulled in and shut the engine off, Judy opened her eyes. She rubbed her face, looked around, and asked, "Where are we?" I pointed to the sign by the restroom entrance that said, *'Welcome to Florida!'*

"Did you drive all night?" She couldn't believe that I hadn't pulled over to rest. I opened the windows, and the warm, fresh air rolled in. I got out and opened her door for her, extending my hand to help her get out after sitting so long. We walked into the restrooms and cleaned up for the last leg of the trip.

Judy had never seen the lizards that seemed to be all over the shrubbery. I watched her try to catch one and then squeal when she managed to grab it, which made me laugh.

We walked around the open yard areas, stretching our legs and talking about what had happened the night before and what we could do once we got to our hotel. I looked at my watch again and realized we had spent nearly an hour there. It wasn't anything like Dorothy Parker's 1931 story, 'Here We Are,' but it was close.

I went back into the bathroom to make sure I could make the four-hour trip ahead of us without stopping. I knew from our trip to California that Judy had a good-sized bladder, and we were off and headed south with Judy at the wheel.

I lay back but kept my eyes open, just in case Judy needed help along the way. I did my best to listen, but I was tired and kept slipping into short periods of sleep. With my eyes closed, I felt her take the freeway that took us to the entrance of the state highway heading toward Orlando. As I drifted off, I felt no hesitation in her driving, and I was napping again within a matter of seconds.

Judy woke me as we came upon a large group of informational signs, and she wasn't sure which one to take. I looked them over and pointed to her exit as we drew closer to it. As soon as we got on the new road, I saw a mileage sign and was eager to see we were only eighteen miles away from our destination. I snapped to attention and pointed her toward which lanes she should use to make the trip smoother.

It seemed to happen much faster than either of us expected, but all of a sudden, there it was - Exit 192, and we could see our hotel from the road. We went up and around the clover-leaf exit and down the surface road to the hotel. Judy was all smiles as she wheeled the car into the hotel parking lot and then parked near the central office.

We walked in together, hand in hand, and saw the sign that said *CHECK-IN 3 pm.* I looked at my watch and saw it was only one o'clock. The desk clerk saw us standing there and asked if she could help us. I gave her my name, and she looked in her books. "Oh, you are our newlyweds from Michigan, aren't you?" Judy nodded shyly, almost blushing. The lady at the desk laughed and called for housekeeping.

She was gone for about two minutes while we stood there, taking in the sights of the hotel. I was impressed with what I saw and squeezed Judy's hand. The front desk clerk came back into the room and motioned us forward. "We had you set to go into a room on the backside of the hotel, but it seems we had a cancellation in one of our smaller honeymoon suites. Would you like that room? There would be no extra charge."

Judy's face lit up as I accepted her offer. I asked if it would be alright if we stayed for fifteen days instead of our original plans to stay a week if I paid her in cash right then. She looked at her room schedule, made some changes, and told me, "I would love to do that for you!" The money we had received during the reception was going to give us an extra week of a honeymoon, and we were ecstatic.

The lady gave me a receipt for my payment and gave us directions to the room. As we started walking away, she called, "Mrs. Greenhoe?" It took Judy a moment to realize that the lady was talking to her. She went back to the desk to see what we had forgotten, and I saw her hand Judy a sign.

As we walked down the hallway, I asked her what it said. I could see her face turn red as she handed it to me. It read: *'Do Not Disturb! Honeymooners Inside!'* I laughed so hard that I nearly fell over. Judy was not amused just then, but she took it home with us when we left.

We finally found the room, and I opened it. I sat our luggage down in the hall and picked her up. She smiled as I took her inside and placed her on the king-sized bed. I brought in all of our luggage and closed the door.

While I was rearranging our belongings, Judy made a show of putting her *'keep out'* sign on the outside doorknob. And what happened next is none of your business!

Learning About Each Other

As much as I worried about Judy having problems with our new intimacy, I think she began to relax and emotionally mature. We spent the next two weeks resting and unpacking our thoughts and burdens. Everyone carries them around, but few people carry as much baggage as the ones who were molested as a child.

We agreed that if one of us needed to interrupt everyday life to talk about something, we would use a simple phrase. When one of us said the phrase, it would bring all else to a halt. Judy used the phrase twice during our stay, and we were able to talk her fears and concerns out, allowing us to get on with our lives. It gave me insight into how she was feeling about herself and thus helped me avoid specific topics until more stable times arrived.

Later in life, I mentioned the 'phrase' contract we had to a man I knew. He couldn't understand why we couldn't just say something like, 'We need to talk!' or my favorite, 'I have a bone to pick with you!' I explained that being confrontational was hard for some people, and it was easier to say something like 'Arabian trolley cars' than to confront someone they loved.

If we promised not to overreact during such sessions, potential problems would be resolved and not allowed to boil under the surface. This person didn't understand that concept, which probably explained why he had been divorced three times. Abrupt might work while you are in traffic, but maybe not as well when you are in love.

We spent our time in the swimming pool, playing mini-golf, hanging out in one of the five restaurants and bars, and walking around the hotel's groomed grass. We spent plenty of time doing the things that newlyweds do, often just lying on our king-sized bed nude and holding hands.

Intimacy is essential, but it involves more than just sex. We used our time to grow comfortable with one another as we were, giving us the emotional closeness that kept our marriage alive for so many decades.

On our third night in the hotel, we lay on the bed, holding hands in the darkness of a warm Florida night. I opened the sliding door a few inches, allowing a soft breeze to waft through, providing us with a calmness that I don't think Judy had ever experienced. We were just happy to be with each other.

In the middle of talking about where we would go the next morning, Judy blurted out our phrase, 'Arabian Trolley Cars,' and then went silent.

I said nothing more, allowing her to say what she wanted to say. We lay there, just holding hands, for nearly five minutes before she finally began to talk.

"I like this sex stuff. I didn't know what to think. I'd heard all the girls at work tell me things, but I didn't know if they were kidding me. You know how some of them are."

Her voice was very soft, but I didn't sense that she was afraid. "I like it when we fall asleep and lie together. I like it when we lie on our sides and you hold my hips. It makes me feel special. Is it wrong to feel special by doing that?"

I was thinking about what I was going to say when she continued. "Do you remember those nights in Los Angeles in that hotel? I so wanted you to lie in bed with me and hold me. But I was afraid of what you would think of me if I asked you to do it."

Sensing she was emptying emotional baggage, I said nothing. I leaned in to kiss her cheek, and she started talking again. "You know, I dreamed about making love with you that night in LA. I wanted to do that with you, but I was afraid of what you would have thought of me."

Judy was lying on her back, her body barely illuminated by the moonlight coming through our windows. She was beautiful in that silhouette.

I turned to my side, put my arm across her abdomen, and just waited. "I didn't want to tease you, but I so badly wanted you to just get into bed with me. You were always the gentleman, and I love you for that. The night we slept in that stupid tent in the desert, it was so hot, but I wanted you to take me then, but I was afraid. You made me feel safe. I have always felt safe with you. Do you know that?"

Judy sighed deeply, and I felt the force of the anxiety as it was leaving her. "Do you know what's weird? Three days before our wedding, Mom pulled me aside to talk to me about sex. I'm 21 and a nurse, and she wants to tell me about sex. Mom should have said something before this, don't you think? So I listened to her, and she told me things that scared me. I had to talk to Lois to make sure that Mom was wrong. That was embarrassing."

Judy turned to her side to face me, then leaned in and kissed me. The moonlight caught her face, and I can remember that moment perfectly. She kissed me again and snuggled into me, making my hand fall to her hips. I pulled her closer to me, just wanting to be as close and comforting to her as I could be.

I heard her sigh again and then heard her whisper, "Did I tell you that you make me feel safe? You do. I was afraid of a lot of things before our wedding, but I'm not afraid anymore."

With no one to see and no clocks to watch, we lay together and kissed. Judy whispered to me about the life she envisioned and wanted for our children. I must have giggled a bit at the mention of children, and she looked and asked me, "What? You don't want children?"

I told her I loved kids and wanted our own, but that would be at least a year later. I watched her smile and agreed.

All night, we lay together, talking and kissing. Everything else could wait. This vacation was our special time together, and I wanted it to be memorable. Judy kept telling me things that concerned her before arriving at the hotel and then explained how that was no longer a problem.

Somewhere during the night, we made love again, and as she lay back, I could see the smile on her face. I asked her what she was thinking about. She looked at me and said, "That was nothing like Mom told me it would be. That was nice. As many times as I thought about doing this with you on our last trip, I'm glad we waited. This is special, and I love you for making it special."

She was right; the night had been special, and Judy was special, something I had already come to realize. As Dad had told me, a woman like her would come along but once in a lifetime. I was glad that I was there to find her. As the sun began to break up the darkness, we drifted off to sleep, still face to face in each other's arms.

You Are Wonderful Tonight

Judy and I enjoyed our time, our surroundings, and each other for the next two weeks. We went to the Atlantic over by Jensen Beach and sat on the beach for several hours, watching the waves on their relentless search for the shore. The rise and fall of the water was hypnotic, and I thought Judy was going to go crazy when a pod of dolphins came into view just off the shore.

We found a small shack that someone was renting out by the night for ten dollars a night or something crazy like that just off the beach. It wasn't much, but we could hear the ocean, and its lullaby of waves made for the perfect background noise. We got up early, returned to the beach for an hour, and then headed west to the Gulf of Mexico near Englewood.

It took about three hours, but we hit the beach there about noon. Judy was astounded by the difference between the ocean and the Gulf beaches. The Gulf of Mexico had some good-sized waves, but nothing like the ocean.

We walked the shoreline and found hands full of black shark teeth in the sand. She was wearing a bright yellow sundress and matching hat that made her look so young and vibrant.

Just before we were getting ready to leave, a man fishing along the shore caught a small ray, which caught Judy's attention. We walked up to watch as he gently removed it from his hook and set it free. The man had seen her watching and allowed her to stroke its skin, leaving her smiling for a long way on our way back.

We stopped to get an ice cream cone from a small shop to help cool down on the way out. Back home, it was about 40 degrees, and the guy on the radio said it was 82 as we left Englewood and headed back to Kissimmee. I couldn't help but smile as Judy talked about all the things we had seen in the past two days.

Judy pulled some of the shark's teeth out of her sundress pocket and sorted through them. She had been telling me about a big tooth she found, and for a moment, she thought she had lost it. She found it in the last handful of teeth, holding it up for me to see. It was huge!

The trip back to the hotel was long, but we were together, and that was all that mattered for now. On our way to the main entrance, the lady who had checked us in greeted us by name and asked if there was anything she could help us find. Judy told her we were doing great and hoped we could go to Disney in the next few days.

The lady's face lit up as she asked me, "Did you get your tickets yet?" I shook my head that we hadn't yet. Her smile got bigger, and she told us to hold up for a moment. She returned and handed me a pair of admission tickets, explaining that they had been found on the lobby floor a month before.

"I don't think anyone is going to claim them now. I was going to give them to someone, and lucky you, they are yours!"

Judy thanked her profusely, and the lady told her she had liked us as soon as she met us that first day and thought we would appreciate them. I assured her we would most certainly make good use of them.

On the way to our room, I remembered I had left my hat on her desk. I opened the room door for Judy and told her I would be right back. Just as I was about to walk to the lobby, I met her as she came to return my hat. I thanked her and was about to head back when she asked me if we had been to Limey Jim's Restaurant and Pub in the lounge. I told her we had not yet made it there but had wanted to visit it before we left.

She held out a pair of tickets redeemable for two drinks per ticket for any night before eight PM. I thanked her again and turned to walk away, but I stopped her one more time to ask, "Why us? Did we win a lottery here that I didn't know we had entered?" I loved the fact that we had gotten them, but this lady had gone above and beyond her capacity as a desk manager.

"You kids looked so darling that first day. It made me feel better about some things that had gone wrong lately. I've watched you walk through here many times, and it seems you two are always smiling. Love is so wonderful when you are young. I hope it stays with you for a long time." She looked both happy and sad at the same time.

I mumbled a heartfelt thanks and asked her name. "My name is Ruth. I've worked here for a long time and see people come and go daily. Few people catch my eye, but you two did as soon as I saw you. You see, my husband died a year ago, and if I had his photo here, you have a stunning likeness to him when he was younger."

I saw her eyes cloud over with that statement.

"Ruth, my wife, and I are indebted to you for your niceties. I'm a medic, and Judy is a nurse, so we understand how rough life can sometimes be. I wish I could do something for you to help repay you for all you have done for us." I saw her eyes cloud with tears, and I just reached out and hugged her there in the hallway.

Working with critically injured or ill people taught me that the human touch is an amazing drug.

I felt her shudder ever so slightly, and she pulled away but still held my hand. I could feel and see the hurt behind her smile, and we just stood there for a moment. Finally, she told me that her break was about over and that she needed to get back to her post.

As we parted, I squeezed her hand and saw her duck into the ladies' room next to the main lobby. I understood why.

I headed back toward our room, knocked just so I wouldn't catch Judy standing in the middle of the room with nothing on, and walked in. A few weeks ago, that would have never happened, but now? It was like she had been doing it all her life.

She asked if I had found my hat, and I held it out. I told her about Ruth and her story, and Judy agreed we had to do something special for her. As I headed for the shower, I told her, "It seems God puts some interesting people in my path."

I took my time in the shower, and when I walked back into the room, Judy was still not dressed and was lying on the bed. She had turned the air conditioner to a lower setting, and it was quite comfortable in the room. I lay down beside her, and we just enjoyed the moment. We had time to do that before we had to return to the world.

I looked at the clock and saw it was about 6:30. "We have some drink and dessert tickets to use. Would you want to use them tonight?" Judy nodded and got up to dress. She had never been a lady who used a lot of makeup. She didn't have a fancy haircut, so she was in a red sundress in a matter of two minutes.

As I walked behind her, my only thought was, 'She's *stunning tonight.*' I took her hand, and we walked out of the room. "So that you know, you look lovely. I can hardly believe that you are my wife." I wasn't sure if she blushed or if it was just the hallway lighting illuminating her face.

Judy's walk and how she carried herself made her simple beauty jump out to people.

As the night went on, a lot of people complimented her looks, and I could tell it made her feel even better about herself. She had never been on the receiving end of a lot of compliments, and she wasn't sure of what to say. I told her to say, '*Thank you!*' She swatted at me, but I knew she loved it.

The pub got busy at about nine o'clock, so we returned to our room and talked about the day's events. When you've never been anywhere, everything is an experience to be enjoyed. I had the luxury of traveling a lot when I was in college, and while this was exciting, Judy had never traveled much. Watching her reactions to everything we did was priceless, and we still had ten days left to go.

I discussed calling home, and Judy quickly told me, "Let 'em stew. They know what we are doing!" We had both called our respective families and employers to tell them we had reached our destination. Judy got Lois on the phone, and while I didn't hear what she was saying, I heard a lot of giggling. *Girls!* I heard her tell Lois to say, '*We love you too, Steve!*' and then they hung up.

Calling collect was expensive back then.

I toyed with the idea of watching the news, but as soon as I turned the television on, Judy walked over and shut it off. I looked at her to figure out why she had done that, only to see her smile. "Get in the shower there, big boy. You've got ten minutes before I come in and scrub you down myself. Now git!"

As I said, *Girls!*

After an hour or so of play had passed, we lay on the bed, still nude. The window was open, and a light breeze was blowing in and across our bodies. Neither of us had spoken for almost twenty minutes before Judy broke the silence. "I just want to live *'happily ever after,'* just like this for the rest of our lives."

At that point, all I could do was smile.

The Days, They Fly By Quickly

The next ten days seemed to disappear, but I still remember them yet today. We spent a day at the new Disney World, covering as much as we could in the day we had set aside for it. The Florida complex was vast compared to the California site. SeaWorld was just down the road, so we also spent a day there.

On our previous cross-country trip, we also visited SeaWorld in the Los Angeles area, and it was nice to discuss their differences. We visited a couple of other small local attractions, but most of our days were spent in the pool and alone.

We knew the time we were enjoying right then would be non-existent once we returned to our jobs. Judy wanted to 'go somewhere.' I finally convinced her that those places would be there for a long time, but we would only be 'new' as we were then but once.

Most of our nights were spent lying next to each other on the king-sized bed, holding hands, talking, kissing, and giggling. One night, Judy asked me, "Why is kissing you now so much different from before we were married?"

As an answer, the comedian in me whispered back to her I had stopped brushing my teeth. Did it make that much of a difference?

Of course, that comment was rewarded with a quick slap on the wrist. It was nice just to be able to be goofing around and giggling at stupid stuff. Yes, we were young adults, but neither of us was that far removed from being teenagers. We had no children to mind, no clocks to punch, and no one to whom we had to answer. For two glorious weeks, we were able to be kids on a honeymoon.

Of course, we spent plenty of time making love or talking about it. We were young and alone, and nature took its course. One late morning, we were 'involved,' and suddenly, there was a light knock on the door with a voice telling us it was 'room service!' Before I could say anything, the maid opened the door, but thankfully, I had set the door chain, and her entry was denied by the backup security chain.

I heard her say something like, 'I'm sorry, I'll come back later!' For a moment, Judy was horrified, but a second later, we were in hysterical laughter about our near miss. When we calmed down a bit, I asked Judy, "What? You didn't put up your 'Honeymooners Within' sign? I'm shocked, shocked, I tell you!" Of course, that set off another ten-minute giggling spell.

I said something about how the guys at the ambulance base would love to hear this story. That response was promptly met with her, 'Don't you dare!'

I told her I wouldn't do that to her, but I might whisper it to Lois and the girls at the hospital, which surprisingly also was not well received. Once I stopped laughing, I whispered to her, "Judy, I think they know what we are doing here. They will quiz you about this stuff, trust me!"

That was how our honeymoon days were spent. Talking, giggling, and lying nude on our bed. It was beautiful, enchanting, and immensely enjoyable. Even the unexpected arrival of Judy's period didn't deter a thing. She was upset, but I assured her that as a graduate of a major college with a degree in the biological sciences, I was well aware of what was happening. Judy was still embarrassed, but I stayed calm, and soon enough, she was over it.

We spent part of that day discussing how we would handle various things in the future. One of our first promises was to be straightforward and honest with each other. We talked about our work and how it would affect us. We decided that when one of us came home, other than a brief 'hello' or 'good morning,' the already-at-home partner would refrain from talking about much until the just-arrived partner had at least half an hour to decompress.

She knew well that my job was a high-stress situation occasionally, and I would come home and sit and think. Conversely, Judy's position in the OB department mostly had its good times, but it had its dark times as well. Death in the ER was one thing, but a death in the OB unit was never expected.

Short of a house fire, we promised never to bother one another until we said the magic three words, 'I love you.' Everything was to be cured with those words. If one of us needed to talk, we would ask for 'a moment.' We pledged always to respect the other's opinions and never carry an argument over to another day.

It may sound dumb and nothing but youthful expectations, but those promises made while naked on a bed in a Florida hotel were to set the tone for the rest of our young lives. In our decades together, I can recall fewer than five serious discussions that, if allowed, could have escalated into a fight. With me, it was always the words of my father that would ring in my ear. 'If it means this much to her, Doc, surrender your argument. She is the best thing that will ever happen to you. Don't ruin it over something stupid.'

As usual, Dad was right.

It was on that bed that we renewed many other vows. We promised never to part without saying the three words. We would also always be honest and upfront with one another. I would not be jealous of men she met in the line of her job, nor would she be upset if she saw me talking to another lady. I alone held the key to Judy's heart, and she kept the key to mine. We would never give the other a reason to doubt each other. Never.

Finally, I promised Judy that no matter what happened, she would be my forever love, and she promised to be mine. In the years that followed, especially as I watched my heart slip away from me, I fought the good fight for her and kept her close to me, protecting her from all things wicked. Some may have thought those promises were the words of teenagers in love, but we held fast to them all our lives.

As the last morning of our stay arrived, we spent one more morning in each other's arms, holding each other tight. It was a time we would never forget. It forever played a part in our lives together. As we checked out, I saw our friend Ruth and stopped her. Judy reached into her bag and brought out a set of 'ears' from the local kingdom with her name embroidered on it. Ruth hugged Judy and then me.

As I said, that stay in Florida set the tone of our lives.

Home Again

The journey home was uneventful despite some slippery roads in the mountains of Tennessee. We weren't in a hurry and made an occasional stop to see something Judy had spotted on a billboard along the freeway.

Most of them were a lot like the old circus 'freak show' banners you used to see back in the Fifties and Sixties - long on hyperbole but short on substance. It was a Tuesday morning, and neither of us had to work until Thursday, so it was just an extension of the journey.

We stopped at a rest area just inside the Michigan border to walk around and prepare for the last two-hour jaunt to home. I counted up my spare change and found enough for a quick call to Steve and Lois to warn them we would be home soon. They wanted to stop and talk about things, but Judy asked them to come over the next day. She explained we were exhausted, and if we could get rested, we would be better able to meet with them. They wished us well and said they would see us tomorrow.

I had driven that same route many times on my trips to Cincinnati and Cleveland, but it seemed to be both longer and shorter than I had remembered. Judy had gotten much quieter than she had been the entire trip, and I asked her if she was alright.

"I'm fine. I'm just beginning to realize that we are about forty-five minutes from the rest of our lives. It would have been nice to be able to stay there another week."

I reached across and put my hand on her knee. "I know, dear. I've thought about that as well. You remember both Disney parks had a 'Land of Tomorrow,' but neither had a 'Land of Forever.' If I could have found that place with you, I'd have never come home. Short of being there, I'm just happy I can spend my time here with you. Do you still love me?"

That was a question we would ask one another at random times throughout our lives. I know it sounds goofy, but it was just something that we did. Habits are like that. When you do something on a steady basis, it became a habit. All through our life, it was one of our habits. It sounded like a question to the casual listener, but it was an affirmation of love to us. That part of the vow said, *'To love and to cherish.'* We were young, but our experiences in matters of life and death were profound.

If I remember right, we rolled into the driveway at about seven o'clock that night. As we walked into the house, I felt the warmth engulf us. I walked in and found a note on the table from Steve that read, *'I lit the furnace for ya, my brother, to be sure your love nest would be warm!'* I showed it to Judy and saw the smile break out that always set my heart sailing.

While Judy arranged some things some friends had placed in the living room, I brought in our luggage. I went into our bedroom, expecting to find the same mess that had been there when we left to go to Florida. Instead, we found our friends had brought in Judy's enormous bed from her old apartment and set it up for us.

Someone, Lois, I suspect, had even put some new sheets we had received for wedding gifts on it. The layers had also been turned down, allowing us to slide into it later that night.

After showering and getting ready for bed, we sat side by side on our couch and stared at an oil painting someone had given us. It was a huge oil painting of sailboats in various shades of blue. It was filled with little optical illusions that invited the viewer to study it at their own pace.

Judy laid her head on my shoulder, and we sat like that for almost an hour, saying nothing verbally. Our only communication was holding hands, and I could feel the love she was sending me via her touch. I was exhausted, but wanted to tell her one more thing before calling it a night.

"Have you ever heard of a guy by the name of Roy Croft? He was a writer and poet back in the Thirties." She never moved from my shoulder but shook her head. "Well, you might not have heard his name, but he had a poem that many people use in their wedding vows. I thought about using it, but I'd heard it a few other times and wanted to say something special about you."

She lifted her head and kissed my cheek. I kissed her back and continued. "I almost used this poem because it was the truth. I think I know it from memory. Let me try it."

I situated myself so I could look into her eyes and began.

I love you not only for what you are
but for what I am when I am with you.
I love you not only for what you
have made of yourself
but for what you are making of me.
I love you for that part of me you bring out.

I must have told that girl a thousand times before that I loved her, but I could see that the words had hit the right emotions this time. I saw the tears forming in her eyes, so I stood up, offered her my hand, and raised her to her feet. We embraced each other for a minute and headed to our official bedroom.

Judy wanted by the wall, so I let her in first and then jumped in myself. We lay on our backs, holding hands and sneaking the occasional kiss. I heard her sigh deeply, but I knew it was out of contentment. Sometime before we fell asleep, she snuggled down. She put her head on my chest and mumbled how listening to my heartbeat made her happy.

Moments later, I heard her breathing become deeper and slower, and I knew she was asleep. Before I fell asleep, I remember thinking about how lucky I had been to find her. My long points were her short ones. Her fortes were my shortcomings. I was gregarious, and Judy was shy, but the two of us made for a well-rounded couple.

Thus, our first night together as husband and wife in our home began for real. For the longest time, we had that *'happily ever after'* life Judy so desperately wanted to live.

Intermission Before the Next Act

As a kid, my father would always tell me these long-winded stories, and I could never figure out why he was telling me those things. Just as he got to the end, he would say to me, *I told you that, so you better understand this.* I didn't always see the point of his long story, but there was a reason I have spent so much time telling you about our romance and honeymoon. I want you to see how we were able to stay so close for so long, even when life went horribly wrong.

In the first part of this story, I have dealt with minutes/hours/days. From here on out, that may still happen occasionally, but now we will probably deal in weeks/months, and maybe even weeks/months/years. Perhaps because of the almost unique closeness that Judy and I enjoyed, I felt her unraveling long before it happened.

You will see times when you might think Judy was weak emotionally, but that was never the case. She was a strong woman. I sometimes worked with her at accident scenes and in the Emergency Room. I had watched her handle accident scenes that had sickened a few of my cohorts, but never Judy. She was a rock, but there seemed to be times when she would become weak emotionally.

Now I know why she appeared weak in her inner strength. I remember when I noticed it when it started to happen. *Now*. I knew something was wrong, but I didn't think it might become as bad as it became. It had to do with some of the issues she developed in her brain over the course of her thirties and forties. It was also one of the anomalies of her brain that led to her stroke 42 years into our marriage.

I will continue the love story, but every love story has an unfortunate turn. Ours was no different.

Years ago, I wrote a novella titled "The Murder of Carrie Greene." Because that story was published nowhere, I can safely tell you the plot.

You'll think it was written about Judy, but this story's plotline was developed in 1972. Its original title was to have been "The Murder of Allen Brown." I changed it around because, then, my target audience readers were women.

Basically, a young and successful lady rises in her profession, which makes many other people upset and envious. Envy is not a pleasant emotion. The title character becomes pregnant, and while on vacation, she miscarries and falls into a deep depression. Her emotional recovery is slow and arduous, but she finally makes a return to her job, seemingly healthy.

In actuality, she was far from 'normal' inside.

Her husband decides they will host a New Year's party, and for the first two hours of the party, 'Carrie' does very well. Unbeknownst to her husband, a very caring and supportive man, someone sent back an RSVP with a nasty note. It read, *'I wouldn't come to your party if it were the last one on Earth. You flaunted your money on that vacation, and you killed your baby. You deserve your pain!'*

In the last scene, Carrie disappears. About the time her husband and her best friend realize she is gone, she appears at the top of a long stairway into the room where everyone is gathered. She can be heard talking to herself, and then produces a pistol and suicides in front of everyone. Her body falls to the ground level, and they discover she is holding the returned note in her hand.

The ending lines of the novella read, *'It was unsigned. Her husband slumped to the floor, weeping; his heart broke, his life gone. Thus had occurred the murder of Carrie Greene.'*

That story does not show how my wife ended up, but I know exactly when, where, and what led to her emotional and physical collapse. It was the only time in my life that I had ever let my wife down, and it cost us both dearly.

Thanks for reading so far. I don't mean to kill the mood here because there are a lot of good things to come, but as I said, every love story takes a wrong turn.

Ours was no different.

Life Becomes Normal

Humans are odd in that they are so willing to face massive changes in their lives and accept new habits as if they had been doing them all their lives. That was the case with us after our wedding. We developed our daily patterns within a week of returning to work. Judy worked the midnight shifts, meaning I had to stay quiet during the day while she slept.

I worked twenty-four and forty-eight-hour shifts, leaving her alone for large chunks of the week. Judy would often visit the base and make some runs with us on her off days. On other days, she would make trips to visit her parents, grandmothers, and the rest of her family and, of course, to see my father. She loved his oddball sense of humor, and she always returned with a bad joke and a big smile on her face.

By the time Steve and Lois were married in July, our routines had settled into a pattern. It stayed much the same for the rest of our lives. I took up my lifelong habit of writing during quiet times when Judy slept and she visited her friends and family when I was at work. On those odd days when we both had a day off together, we tried to do something that would make us both happy and get us out of the house.

About fifteen months after our wedding, Judy said she wanted to talk to me again about our future. We were sitting in the shade of a giant oak tree near a small lake, tossing the occasional pebble into the water and kissing. Throughout our lives, we made it a practice to kiss, even in public. It wasn't an attempt to make a *'public display of affection'*; it was another renewal of our vow *'to love and to cherish.'*

We had seen several friend's marriages fall apart over stupid and petty things, and we didn't want that to happen. We would remember lying together that moonlit night in Florida, always vowing to care for and respect each other. With each kiss, we renewed that vow. I know it sounds weird to some, but it worked for us for over forty-six years.

Just as we had pulled back from such a kiss, Judy said our phrase, signifying that she wanted to talk about something serious. The 'phrase' thing was another vow we had made in the darkness of a Florida night, and we used it with all due solemnness. I waited for her to speak. We were watching a flock of ducks swimming along the shore of the lake. It was a beautiful sight.

When she whispered to me, "I want to have a baby. I think we are ready," my initial reaction was, *'Are you crazy?'* I didn't move or physically react, but I knew she was observing my body language. I turned to face her on the blanket and studied her face. She reached out for my hand and said it one more time. "I want to have a baby."

Her grip on my hand tightened as she waited for my response. I hadn't told her about it, but had thought along those same lines a few months back. We had picked up a pregnant woman who was in full labor. We had gotten her to the hospital with five minutes to spare. I could have delivered the baby, but it was a risky thing to do in the back of a moving ambulance.

Besides the obvious risks, there was always the possibility of an infection in a less-than-sterile environment. There was a standing joke about cleanliness versus sterility. The correct response was that the only thing sterile in the back of an ambulance was possibly the attendant. It was impossible to keep a unit that housed a road accident one hour and then picked up an injured farmer the next hour *'sterile.'* You settled for *'as clean as possible.'*

"Alright." I gathered myself." Have you seen your doctor about this? Get some blood work done to make sure you are in your best physical health, and then I am all for it." Judy almost threw herself into my arms and hugged me. "Hey, now! You get that physical first! No shortcuts!" She knew what I meant, but she slapped me anyway.

As she leaned over my shoulder in our embrace, Judy whispered to me she was afraid I wouldn't want to have a baby. My answer to her was simple: "It's instinctive to want to be a mother. It tells me that your emotions have accepted your surroundings and that you feel we are safe and secure together. It also tells me you love me." Her embrace told me she was ready.

We spent the rest of the day talking about what it would take to be ready in every way possible to be parents. Judy knew I had been abused as a child. During that honeymoon vacation, we had spoken about that situation. I made her my promise that kind of behavior would stop with me and that just as I would never abuse her, I would never hurt our child. We kissed on that, and she believed me.

After dinner that night, we sat in the darkness of our living room. The windows were open, a local radio station playing quietly in the background, and we talked long into the night. Although we were alone, our words were whispered, perhaps to signify the respect and understanding of our monumental decision.

Or maybe it was because we both had a bit of apprehension. Making a baby was easy. Raising a child was a lifetime effort.

By the time we made our way to bed, we had decided that as long as Judy was healthy enough to do the pregnancy thing, we would try it. She told me she had already talked to one of the OB doctors there and could get an appointment later in the week. We kissed on it and fell asleep with a child's lullaby dancing through our minds.

True to her word, Judy set up a physical and was given a clean bill of health to become pregnant. She had put away her birth control pills in late August, with the idea that conception would be possible and safe beginning in January. In the meantime, we used other 'cautionary methods,' and life went onward.

Thanksgiving Day family dinners came and went, and snow flew in early December that year. Steve and I attended many accidents, several of which were fatal in the first week as people learned to drive again on the slippery roads. One such crash claimed the lives of two little boys. I will tell you here and now something that all medics and ER nurses learn quickly. You can claim to be unaffected by those things all you want, but those who have also done the job would know that you are a liar.

Steve and I had found emotional comfort in our talks at home for over five years. Now that he was also married, we found consolation with our wives. It was a necessary and natural process that kept you from losing your mind. Many war veterans didn't have anyone to help them unpack the traumas that they had witnessed while abroad. They didn't want to talk to people who had never been on a battlefield once they got home, either. The effects of that kind of isolation were horrific.

On nights like the one when our unit had lost those little boys, Judy and I would lie in the bed together. I put my head upon her breast, allowing my emotions to flow away from me. She was aware of what was happening because her job wasn't always happiness and baby balloons. On the days and nights following a stillborn, I would provide her the same no-questions-asked safe harbor she was giving me.

'To have and to hold from this day forward, for better or for worse, for richer, for poorer, in sickness and in health, to love and to cherish; from this day forward until death do us part.'

Those words ruled our lives. We had made a pact in the moonlight of a Florida night and we vowed to live by them, and we did.

Somewhere during that night, emotions led to kissing, which led to passions flaring, and without ever any planning, we made love for what seemed the longest time. Alternative methods never came to mind. Our motive was to soothe the deep emotional pain, and with the darkness of the night, all was made right in the arms of my wife. It was a Thursday night at the end of the last week of November.

A few weeks later, we were making plans on how to fit our Christmas holiday activities with our various families in our schedules. I had made a fried egg and two slices of toast for both of us, and we were talking at the table. I was in the middle of giving Judy the time slots my dad intended to hold his dinner when she interrupted me. "Whew! Are you sure that egg was good?"

My head turned around and reached for her hand. "Did it make you sick? Did you eat any of it?" She shook her head and pushed her plate away, and I could see she hadn't touched it. I stood up, pulled Judy to her feet, and hugged her as hard as I dared. "You are pregnant! *I know it.* You are pregnant!" She shook her head, telling me that no way could that be possible.

As it turned out, I was right. If you worked at a hospital in the 70s and hadn't been a dork to everyone, you could get some testing done without a doctor's order. Friends being friends and all, the lab people would help you out.

I took Judy to the hospital, where she used that shy little smile that she had used to hook me to get one of the male lab guys to do a blood pregnancy test. Ten minutes later, we found out that we were about to be parents.

There is no way I can find the right words to explain how we felt after finding out the joyous news, but suffice it to say that we were thrilled. We weren't that far from my dad's place, and we drove out to make him the first to know of our joy. I can't remember a time I had ever seen my father cry, but after Judy told him he was about to be a grandfather, I saw him weep in happiness.

Naturally, on the way home, we stopped in to see Steve and Lois, and we danced and jumped together, arm in arm, with a lot of hugging following the dancing. Judy made Lois promise not to say anything at work just yet, but you know one girlfriend can't help but spread the good news of another.

When she went to work that night, the department was filled with balloons and handmade signs of congratulations. The ladies working small OB units in small hospitals were always close-knit. There was a lot of chatter and rib pokes of '*How did **this** happen?*' until someone asked Judy what her mom had said when she had told her.

The problem was, we hadn't told her just yet.

We were going to have Christmas on Judy's side of the family that weekend. She hoped to pull her mom aside, tell her quietly, and hope for the best. I had volunteered to tell her, but Judy gave me that *'Are you nuts?'* look, and I took that as my cue to be quiet.

I had argued that we had been married for two years and that they had to have wondered when you might give them a grandbaby. Judy gave me another look, and again, I realized I was out of my league and should be quiet and take a seat on the bench.

The Sunday we were driving to that dinner, Judy worried and fretted the entire trip up to their home. She was unsure of what she was going to say and how her mom would react. I assured her that, given time, virtually every mother looked forward to becoming a grandmother. I told her we would weather any storm and would be happy about it. Judy wasn't as confident about it as I was.

Just as we walked into her parents' house, we were met by everyone who gave us happy hugs. As it was getting quiet again, the phone rang, and her mom answered it. As soon as I realized it was going to take her a few minutes to get off the call, I handed Judy a pad of paper and a pen, made a scribbling motion, and pointed to her mom on the phone.

She looked at me and shook her head. *'No way!'* but I made the scribble motion again and whispered that it was a perfect time. Judy sighed, wrote out the note, and headed toward the kitchen, where her mom was using the kitchen phone. From a safe distance, I saw her hand the paper to her mom and the look on her face as she read it. Judy was on her own from there.

Without asking my wife if it was all right, I took it upon myself to talk to her dad. As I got him to step out into the garage, I could see Judy's apprehension building as she stood there next to her mom.

Once I was in the garage alone with her dad, I just told him, "Dad, I wanted to tell you that Judy and I are expecting our first baby next August. I hope you approve." Her Dad was a big guy, an oil worker for many years, and then a factory worker, so he was very solid.

He looked at me for almost a full minute. "Is Judy happy?"

I nodded and told him, 'Yes, sir. Very.'

"Are you happy?"

I shook my head and repeated my words, 'Yes, sir. Very.'

He reached for my hand, but hugged me instead. "Does her mother know yet?" I explained Judy had just handed her a note while she was on the phone. He gave a small chuckle and told me, "Good move."

He went into the kitchen with me on his heels. He walked up to the phone, took it from his wife, and told whoever she had been talking with that she would have to call her back and hung up the receiver.

"Woman? Your daughter gives you a note telling you she is having a baby, and you can't hang up to hug her? What the hell? Hug her. Tell her you are proud of her because I damn sure am proud of her." He reached out to Judy and hugged her tight. I was never entirely sure, but I sensed that a tear of happiness formed in his eye for just a moment.

The rest of the dinner was one of the happiest I can ever remember spending with them. Judy's dad made several calls, and soon, other relatives arrived to congratulate us on our baby. The comedian in me wanted to tell them it had been my pleasure, but I doubted they would have laughed. Instead, we had a nice dinner and family get-together, and our ride home was a dream.

As we lay in bed that night, we held each other for the longest time. We talked about names and cribs, remembered, and re-pledged our vows to one another. It was a night of great joy, and somewhere in the background, as we drifted off together, the radio station was playing the Christmas song, 'Joy to the World.' I kissed my wife, and we fell asleep.

'Momma's Baby'

Judy's first obstetrical visit wasn't until late February, but she had been talking with the doctor she had chosen almost every night at work. I had known this lady for a long time myself, working with her several times when we had imminent deliveries out in the field. She had a sense of humor and was easygoing, something we wanted in her doctor.

While the office nurse was surprised to see me at her first official exam, the doctor wasn't and made me feel like part of the entire situation. When she was through, she told us that Judy was in excellent condition and that she could foresee no potential issues for her pregnancy. She told me I was welcome to come with Judy any time I wanted to attend, as long as Judy didn't mind.

Judy asked how long the doctor felt it was safe for her to work. "As long as you don't develop any problems along the way, that will be up to you. You are young and in great shape. It will help to have an informed and involved husband." She smiled at me, and I thanked her. I was in that rare group of men who wanted to be in the delivery room back then. Not only was it not universal, but many hospitals also prohibited it.

We left the office with a couple of prescriptions for vitamins and some other medication I'd long since forgotten. We headed out to grab lunch at one of our favorite haunts. I remember giggling at the way Judy was almost floating around the room. It was nice to see my lady so happy. Even the waiter noticed her attitude and said something like, 'You seem happy!' Judy thanked him, but I had to tell him, "We just found out that she is going to be a momma!"

Everyone who heard me talking leaned in to congratulate us. One older lady stopped on her way out to wish us nothing but happiness and kissed Judy on the back of her hand. Once the table was quiet, we giggled a bit, and we finished our meal. When I went to pay for it, the manager told me it was on the house to say 'congrats.' We both thanked him and headed to the car.

I was supposed to be at work, but I had one of my partners fill in for me so I could be with Judy. As it turned out, the guys at the base would be extremely involved in Judy's care, but more on that later. We drove home, happy and content that all was going to go well. Once back in the house, I had about an hour to kill before I had to return to work, so we just lay on the bed together, laughing, kissing, and giggling.

Before I left to go back to work, we made another vow to each other. We both knew of the stress a pregnancy could bring into a new relationship, so we promised to give the other extra respect and space needed to keep ourselves stable. I vowed to help Judy do some of 'her' chores without her asking. She promised to be extra tolerant of me as her hormones played havoc with her. We'd both seen it in others and didn't want that in our relationship. We kissed on it and said, 'I love you' in unison, and I was gone.

Time Marches On

Judy became even more radiant as winter turned into spring and summer. Motherhood suited her perfectly; it was easy to see her joy as her belly grew. Of course, she had discomfort, but there are burdens in life that you don't mind carrying. Her doctor visits continued to be perfect, and each report showed that the baby was growing just as expected.

Somewhere along the line, they had done a scan of some type, and we got a little x-ray-like photo where we could see our baby. I held it up to the light and pointed it to it, and told Judy, "There's our little Bozo!" Until the moment our daughter was born, she was called 'Bozo.' Judy would call me from work to talk about something, and I would ask about 'Little Bozo.' Many people thought us nuts, but we were having the time of our lives.

Then came the day that Judy scared me to the verge of tears. I was at work, roughly ten blocks from our home, when she called me, telling me to come home right away. Not knowing what was happening, my partner and I jumped into the ambulance and flew back with the lights and sirens running.

When we pulled up, Judy was sitting on a porch swing, smiling at us. Mark, my partner for the day, and I both jumped out, carrying our portable jump bags with us. "Judy, what's wrong? What happened?" I don't mind telling you, but I was scared out of my mind.

Mark and I stood there, waiting for her to 'point to where it hurt' when she smiled. "Give me your hand." She took my hand and laid it on her belly. For several seconds, I felt nothing, and then it happened. Bozo kicked me. She looked up at me, and her smile grew even bigger while I started crying.

It is hard to define that moment when your baby first tells the world, 'Hey! I'm here!' I fell to my knees and kept my hand still, and it kicked again.

Judy took Mark's hand and placed it on her belly next to mine for about a split second before she kicked again. His face beamed a huge smile. Judy and Mark talked about the kicking, but I was utterly overwhelmed. I placed my forehead on her belly, closed my eyes, and sobbed each time I was kicked by the baby. I can't describe the thoughts that ran through my head for the next three minutes as little Bozo 'voiced' her displeasure at my pressure.

Radio traffic on our unit radio finally made me gather myself. It wasn't for us, but I knew it could be for us at any minute. I stood up, went into our home, and washed my face in cold water so I was at least presentable should we get called out. I heard our dispatch talking to Mark while I was inside, so I hurried along as best I could.

I looked at Mark first, but he shook me off and pointed to my wife. As much as I loved that woman, my love for her tripled that day. As I held her and kissed her, my eyes were tearing up again. My heart raced at what the two of us had done. We had seen the picture of the baby, but I had just felt it make us realize she was there and wanted attention.

I heard Mark jump into the rig, and the big door on the unit slammed shut. I held Judy tighter for a moment and whispered, 'I love you so much!' in her ear. Her face was filled with a light I had never seen on her before, making it hard for me to leave, but I knew I had to get moving. We kissed once more, said our three words, and I was back in the unit.

I apologized to Mark for my breakdown of emotions, and he told me, "Man! I would have done the same as that. That was awesome! I can't even begin to know how you feel. That's got to be special." Mark was one of the few guys I knew I thought even had a chance of having a relationship with a lady as I had found with Judy.

Mark would soon become my new partner. Just then, we had no clue that Steve's family would shortly have a tragedy that would require him to move nearly a thousand miles away within the month. Saying goodbye to my longtime partner, my brother-in-arms was one of the saddest days of my life. We built a special relationship after seven years of working, living, and getting married a few months apart.

We had been through it thick and thin. The cops started calling us 'The Dynamic Duo.' One of the sergeants told us he had never seen a pair of medics work so closely together, staying calm under gunfire, finishing our tasks, and laughing later. He had been in Vietnam and had some experience of what being in the thick of stuff was about, and he respected us. I'm not saying that our work was as dangerous as in an actual war, but the two of us would come under gunfire several times as partners.

As we wheeled back into the base, Mark and I just sat in our seats. I thanked him again for being so supportive of Judy and me. He grinned and told me it wasn't a problem. About the time we opened the doors of the unit to go back inside, I saw one of the other guys pull into our small parking lot. I thought maybe he had forgotten something, and I held the door open for him, and he came into the living quarters with us.

I asked him what he was doing hanging around two known criminals, and he told me he was there to replace me. I looked at him and then at Mark and saw his big guilty smile get wider. "Boss, I know you are just aching to get back there with your darling wife and your baby, so I called Dick to see if he could wander in to cover for you." As I said, my crew was to play an essential role in 'our' pregnancy.

I thanked the guys, and then I was gone. Judy was surprised to see me, but I could tell that she was happy to see me. We sat on the porch swing, talking about nothing, waiting for Bozo to kick again. If someone were to ask me to explain the emotion I felt that day, I couldn't do it. It was one of the most intense moments of my life, and it left me unable to talk and even think. I was going to be a father!

The Dog Days of Summer

Dr. Adams, Judy's OB doctor, had put her due date on roughly August 26th in the middle of a blistering hot summer. I was incredulous that she kept smiling and working during that kind of heat. I'd never been one for air conditioning, but I bought a slightly used one from my neighbor to make her as comfortable as possible. It wasn't the best cooling unit, but it helped her rest a little better.

Our trips to see the doctor became closer and closer together as the last week of August approached, but Judy showed no signs of going into labor. Eventually, her due date came and went, and Judy was still going to work every day. Every time her OB doc came to deliver a baby to someone else, she would talk for a moment with Judy.

Over Labor Day weekend, Dr. Adams decided that if Judy didn't deliver the baby by the fifteenth of the month, she would induce her with medications. Judy wasn't thrilled by that idea, but her belly was becoming bigger by the day, and she was getting very uncomfortable. She rarely complained, but it was quite understandable that she was in pain. I did what I could at home, but back rubs and cold cloth applications would only do so much for her.

On the morning of September 6th, Judy began to experience small contractions. Still, her OB experience told her they were just 'practice contractions,' better known in the medical field as Braxton-Hicks contractions. I was scheduled to work the next two days and arranged to have her sleep at the ambulance base with me.

Judy had the sixth and seventh off, but was scheduled to work the morning shift on the eighth. She spent most of the day at home on Thursday, the seventh of the month, but she drove over to the base around five o'clock. As soon as she walked in the door, Mark and I both knew her active labor had begun.

Judy found the chair in which she felt most comfortable and did her best to relax. She had coached hundreds of women through this part of labor, and we had taken the Lamaze course. For the first couple of hours, I was doing the exercises with her, but she warned me she could be in active labor for another day or so. I was pretty sure that concept didn't thrill her, and I knew it wasn't what I wanted to hear either.

Mark and I began switching on and off with the exercises and getting her to relax and rest when the opportunity came around. Judy was hanging tough and remained calm for much longer than I probably could have. Around ten o'clock that night, the contractions had slowed considerably, and I talked her into taking a shower. Given a choice, she decided I should be the one with her in the shower, much to Mark's relief.

I had gotten her in the shower area, undressed, and she was just about to step into the shower when her water broke. Fortunately, I had stripped down to only my underwear with the idea that I would be there to support her in the shower, saving my shoes. We had a small chair in the room, so I placed it in the shower, allowing her to sit and relax as much as possible.

I stepped out for a moment to tell Mark what had just happened, and I thought I heard him tell me, "I'm on it, Boss!" He was from somewhere down south and called everyone 'Boss.' I found it rather neat, but as I went back into the shower to tend to my wife, I wasn't exactly sure what he might 'be on.' I jumped into the shower, helped Judy cool down, and washed her hair. She had been hot and sweaty, and I thought it might help her or at least make her feel better.

When I finally got her up and dressed as much as she was going to be for a couple of days. I carefully walked her back out to the living quarters to see that Dick, one of our fellow medics. Mark had asked him to stop over the fill-in for me. He helped Mark move Judy to her seat again, and I took advantage of that time to get dressed.

When I returned, my guys were helping Judy work through a new style of contractions that signaled that her real labor had started. I knelt to talk with my wife, asking her how she was doing. Mark said she was doing fine and that I should rest while I could. He promised me he and Dick would handle everything until Judy told them she felt we should head to the hospital. I looked at her to make sure that she was alright with that plan, and she nodded. I kissed her, reminded her I loved her and went to bed. It was ten-thirty.

I remember nothing until Mark came into the bunk area and woke me. "Boss, your lady says you need to get to the hospital. She's doing good, but her contractions are down to less than six minutes." The 'six-minute' business startled me, but Judy was still calm and working with the guys as her labor increased. I was impressed with her calmness. I'm not sure I would have stayed as calm.

I grabbed her bags, jumped into my 1968 Camaro SS, and brought it up to the door. Dick and Mark carefully led her out to the car, opened her door, and helped her into the seat. Mark had even brought out a thick towel for her to sit on. I laughed as he said, 'Just in case she makes a mess in your nice car, Boss!'

My friends had thought of everything.

Before they could shut the door, Judy pulled them in, one by one, kissed them on the cheek, and thanked them for helping her with her labor. A bigger bunch of 'aw, shucks, ma'am' couldn't have been found within one hundred miles. I asked them to call the OB department and tell them that Judy wouldn't be at work the next morning, but would be in shortly. They said they would call immediately. They were some great guys.

The hospital was about fifteen miles away, but the roads were clear, and I pressed the 327 motor in the Camaro to hurry along a little faster. Within twenty minutes, a man from the ER was pushing her into the hospital in a wheelchair.

The longtime OB nurse officially became a patient.

Once in the OB department, Judy was surrounded by her co-workers, putting on her name tag, starting her IVs, drawing blood, and checking her for dilation and effacement. It was two in the morning when they called Dr. Adams and gave her an update on my wife.

Judy had done well at home. Her initial check for dilation showed she was already at eight centimeters. The doctor told them she would be right in to prepare for the delivery.

I stayed with Judy, talking with her when I could and coaching her when she needed it. I could hear another woman screaming somewhere else in the department, but Judy had remained calm to that point. Dr. Adams came into the room, spoke with us for a moment, did her exam, and then told the staff that it wouldn't take long.

When she came back, she scrubbed up as she walked and asked me, "Weren't you going to do the delivery?" Judy and I had talked to her about the possibility of me assisting, but I had never heard a definite answer. I told her I would love to deliver my child, and she smiled and waved me to return with her. I kissed my wife and followed the doctor to the scrub area.

We were gone for almost ten minutes, but Judy was nearly out of control when I returned. One of the girls told me she had begun to lose it within a minute of me leaving the room. I hadn't even considered that Judy would lose it so fast this late in the game. I slipped to her side and whispered in her ear. I told her I was back, that I loved her, and that she needed to slow down and work with me again.

Within a minute, Judy began to calm down, with only the occasional moan. The nurse beside me said, "You have to show me how you did that!" Years of holding hands, midnight talks, and whispering 'I love you' to her had allowed me to reach that inner Judy. I told her the professional persona needed to step out and be active in this delivery. Amazingly, she got there just in time.

At about 3:50 am, something in Judy began to work to expel the baby inside her. The baby's head twisted to the proper angle, and her contractions started in earnest. I had assumed a position between her legs to make the delivery, with Dr. Adams standing just behind me, watching every action at every moment. I told Judy that I wanted her to listen to me and me alone. "Just concentrate on my voice and nothing but my voice. We can do this, Judy. We can do this."

One of her nursing colleagues was at her head, helping her with sitting up, pushing, and then relaxing. I took my directions from her and passed them on to my wife in the calmest voice I could muster. Inside, my guts were quivering with excitement and the fear I might do something wrong and hurt our child. I had done this many times before, but it was my baby in my hands this time.

I kept a running monologue of what Judy should do, assuring her she was doing great. Almost unnoticed at first, the mechanics of her body that I knew signaled an imminent delivery went into motion. My baby's head made its first appearance to the world and then pulled back. I reached up to push back on its head to keep it from being expelled too explosively and felt the pressure of a contraction pushing it forward.

After a couple of contractions, I eased up to allow it to descend out of the birth canal until its head was entirely delivered. Almost like an old-fashioned cuckoo clock, the head turned from facing down to a nearly perfect ninety-degree rotation, looking at her momma's thigh. In the next contraction, Dr. Adams whispered for me to lift the infant's head to allow the lower arms to clear Judy's body.

I heard her whisper, 'Good job!' in my ear as I pushed down on the baby, clearing the upper shoulder and arm. I had done this before, but I fully admit that as I gripped the slippery little body and braced for the final contraction, every nerve in my body was on fire. Sometimes, it was a slow exit, and sometimes, that last push was like a major league fastball, low and outside.

As calmly as I could muster, I implored her one more time. "Come on, Judy, rest for a second, then give me one more big push. You can do this, dear. I know you can do this. You are almost done." I heard the nurse tell her to take one last deep breath and then push again. I heard Judy help the contraction and then felt my baby slide into my hands.

We had decided not to be told what our child would be, so my first instinct was to look and tell my wife, "Judy! It's a girl!" As I was telling her that, I noticed the umbilical cord wrapped around its neck. Without ever really thinking about it, I flipped it over her head, allowing her to slide freely into my arms.

I don't recall doing it, but I must have gone into my little zone of happiness, becoming oblivious to everything around me. As I stared at her, I swear her bright blue eyes looked into mine with a knowing look far beyond what her life's first few minutes should have given her.

My little bubble was finally broken when Dr. Adams told me to lay the baby on Judy's stomach carefully. I knew I had to do that, but my emotions overtook me. "Why don't you go up there and give your wife a big kiss for doing such an excellent job? You both did just fine."

I think the doctor just wanted to get me out of the way as diplomatically as she could so she could see what might need to be repaired. I was more than happy to hand off to her so I could make my way to her face and kiss my wife. She hugged me as I looked in from her shoulder, and both of us cried in our happiness. I cut the umbilical cord just seconds before a nurse whisked her off to be cleaned up, weighed, measured, and footprinted. As the nurse left the delivery room with our baby girl, I exclaimed to her, "Her name is Amanda, Amanda Dawn!"

It was exactly four o'clock.

Several minutes later, Amanda was brought back to us in a tightly wrapped blanket and handed to Judy. I saw the tears well in her eyes as she made a quick visual inspection. The nurse who had taken her out to be cleaned up told us, "Little Miss Amanda Dawn weighs eight pounds and eight ounces. She is just shy of twenty-one inches long and is perfect in every way I can tell. Dr. Adams will do another exam on her in a few minutes, but for now, she's yours."

Judy kissed Amanda's cheek, and immediately, her little lips searched for something to eat. Another nurse helped Judy put her to her breast, and within a matter of seconds, the sound of her sucking filled the room. While we were watching and talking to each other, Dr. Adams made a clean delivery of the placenta and repaired one small tear inside Judy.

She came beside us and congratulated us on a smooth delivery. "I see nothing to worry about with Judy. She did a good job, and everything went as perfectly as possible. I'm going to wash up here, and then I will quickly assess Amanda." As she left the room, she patted me on the shoulder. "You did good, Daddy; you did good!"

Someone brought in a stool for me to sit on, and I realized how tense I must have been. I also knew how tired Judy must have been after nearly a full day of contractions and precious little sleep. Another nurse came in and pried a very upset Amanda away from Judy's breast to take her into a nearby room to be checked out.

I waited for that door to close and kissed Judy's face. I never saw who brought it in, but a cold cloth appeared next to me, so I gently wiped away the sweat from the face of my darling wife. Judy's legs were returned to the bed from the delivery stirrups, and she was about to be wheeled back to her room. I was amazed when she asked if she could walk back.

There was a brief back-and-forth, but there we were, Judy, walking, slowly and haltingly, to be sure, but still under her own power. Her IV pole became a crutch, and I held her from the other side. By the time we reached her room, Judy was exhausted, but still smiling. She was assisted into the bed, her railings raised, and we talked until the doctor returned.

"As far as I can see, you have a healthy little girl who is upset that we interrupted her breakfast. Someone will bring her back in a few minutes. I'd like you to nurse her for a few minutes from each breast and then get some sleep." I heard Judy mumbling something resembling words, so I thanked the doctor for everything. She was exhausted and doing her best to stay awake.

I stayed in the room with her for the next eight hours. I alternately wiped her face with cold clothes, fed her some ice chips, and stroked her face as she slept. Various nursing personnel were in and out of the room, checking IVs, watching for excessive uterine bleeding, and monitoring her vitals. All was going just as it should, and I was relieved.

Somewhere in that blur of time, Judy's parents came to visit, and my father came in, along with three or four others whose names and identities elude me now. Everyone congratulated us on our beautiful baby, telling me it looked like 'Aunt May, Aunt Emily, or some other aunt I hadn't heard about yet. I thought she looked exactly like my daughter.

Just shy of noon, I got ready to go back home because I had to finish my shift. Dick may have been kind enough to come in to cover for me for a while, but it was a Friday night, and Dick and his wife were party animals. I was about to kiss Judy lightly when she awoke. We spoke for a few minutes, and I filled her in on the comings and goings so far. More importantly, I explained Amanda was perfect.

The OB nurse had been in to nurse with her a time or two, but she had been out of it for anything other than a quick 'snack and git' visit. Judy apologized, but I assured her that all was well and that I was proud of her. We held hands as she asked me how she had done during the delivery. "You did wonderful, dear lady. Absolutely wonderful. Everyone was proud of you."

I had one eye on the clock and one on my wife's face. I finally explained to her that while I hated to leave just then, Dick had done us a huge favor by coming in early for me, and I needed to get back. She held her arms out to me, pulled me in for a big hug, and whispered our three words. As I pulled away, I repeated them back to her.

As I walked to the door, I whispered again. "Rest, Judy. We have a lot ahead of us. Rest."

Before I was out of the room, Judy was sleeping again. I stopped at the nurse's station and asked them to keep her visitors to a bare minimum until she was awake on her terms. I made it to the hospital exit doors to the parking lot and walked out. It had been hot the day before, but a massive wave of heat hit me square in the face.

On the way home, I thought about the events of the night and couldn't help but smile. I was thankful that my sweating was hiding my tears of joy. Some gal on the radio was telling me it was 102 outside, and I had no problem believing her. I was happy to get back to the base and get inside.

The guys were all interested in all the details of the birth. That was everyone except Dick, who had to take off. As he headed out the door into the heat, he yelled out, "It's been quiet all night. Maybe you can get some sleep! Congrats, big guy. Next time you talk to Judy, tell her I love her!"

Somehow, I knew he had just cursed us.

New For Old

I had barely had time to shower, change into a clean uniform, and then sit down to talk with Mark when we were signaled that we had a call. Both of us cursed Dick's name as we ran to the garage and out the door. It was stifling outside as we stayed in the drive for a moment, listening for directions to the incident.

The dispatcher told us to head west and then north on a new freeway being built about five miles away. As we got on our way, she told us about a man found unconscious at the work scene. In perfect unison, Mark and I said, "Heatstroke!" It was still over 100 degrees, and working on hot new black asphalt was going to make the working surface well over 110 degrees.

As I had come home from the hospital, I had seen the work crew and was able to direct Mark to the scene. We were on location in less than five minutes, and members of the highway team led us to a large poplar tree on the east side of the new freeway. We found him lying in the shade, barely breathing. One touch of his skin told me he was extremely overheated and wasn't sweating, which was always a dangerous combination.

As I stripped him of as many clothes as possible, Mark ran back to the ambulance and brought back the stretcher and some bottles of fluid. Some of the highway workers helped him carry everything to their fallen friend. As we were placing the man on the cart, his supervisor told me that the guy had been complaining that he didn't feel well for nearly an hour. The boss told him to sit under the tree and rest because the day was almost complete.

I didn't want to scold him there, but I later told him that anytime it was as hot as it was that day, anyone who wasn't sweating was going to get ill, just as their friend had done. The human body secretes fluids mainly to control its internal temperature. Sweat causes the skin to cool, thus releasing body heat.

As soon as we got the stricken man on the cot and strapped down, Mark opened a bottle of fluid and poured it over the man's body. Once we had him in the back of the rig, I wet down a cloth, wiped his face, and wet his hair to lower the temperature of his brain. It was a ten-minute ride to the hospital, and I had poured two more liters of fluid on him.

I tried to get vital data on him, but his heart was racing too fast for me to count his pulse, and I couldn't find a noticeable blood pressure. Even with all the fluids we had used on him, his skin was very hot. I studied his face and saw he was extremely young. Later in the ER, I found out that he had just had his twenty-first birthday a week before.

Once he was in the ER, one of the nurses took a rectal temperature on the man and got a reading of 108.4 degrees. Everyone knew that the young man's chances of surviving were virtually nil. The doctor ordered an EEG, a test to check his brain activity. I had only seen a few such tests, but the brain had shut down from the heat it had absorbed. It wouldn't be long before the body was following the brain. The doctor ordered cold water enemas, but it was a futile attempt.

Another emergency had just walked in through the ER doors, and the staff left me to watch the man run down the remaining time of his life clock. I rarely showed much, if any, emotion in the hospital, but I got the curtains closed just in time to hide my tears. Less than ninety minutes before, I was on an emotional high that followed the birth of my daughter. Now, I was watching a young man in the throes of death over something completely avoidable.

I wasn't allowed to 'pronounce' death, but when his heart tracings stopped, I grabbed the doctor and reported to him that it was my opinion that the man had ceased to be alive. I was not legally allowed to say that he was dead, but he most definitely wasn't alive. It was a game of semantics. The doctor stopped in the cubicle and listened to his chest. He found no heart activity. After looking at his watch, he gave me a time that I was supposed to provide to the charge nurse for the official time of death.

On my way to the ER nursing station, I found a young woman holding a relatively newborn baby standing there. I didn't work for the hospital, but I asked her if I could do anything to help her. "I was told my husband was brought here. He fainted while he was working on the freeway. Could you please tell me where I can find him?"

I never knew if I visibly reacted to her question, but I told her to have a seat in a room just off to the side, and someone would be right with her. My stomach felt queasy as I waited for the ER doc to roll by me again. "Doctor? The wife of that young man in cubicle four is here. She has a new baby." He stopped for a moment and looked at me. It's rare when an ER doctor displays compassion, but I saw the dismay on his face as he looked at me.

He pulled me into the curtained area where the body of the highway worker lay. "Are you alright, son? I was going to congratulate you on the birth of your baby - a girl, I think I heard? This work can be brutal and poorly timed." He shook my hand and told me he was sorry about my having to be the one who spoke with the wife. "I'll go handle that. You need to get out of here. I will take it from here."

I exited through a door that few people knew was there, and I was in the ambulance in less than a minute. Thankfully, Mark was on top of his job, and we were set to roll by the time I got there. I don't know if Mark had seen what was going on, but he said nothing on the way home. We gassed the unit, did a quick supply check, shut the garage doors down, quietly walked into the living quarters, and sat down.

"Mark, have you ever noticed that the balance scales we always seem to work with always insist upon being balanced? My daughter is born, and that man dies. That guy we picked up after that minor fender bender last week died, and the guy two days later lives through some of the worst accident injuries I've ever seen, and that's saying a lot. For every gain, there has to be a loss. Today, it was my gain, and someone else lost." I just shook my head.

Mark wasn't Steve, but he did a darn good job of filling in for him. We talked for almost an hour about the delicate balancing act of life, to which we always had a front-row seat. Life demanded balance, and we saw both ends of the skit that day. Eventually, I was able to shake off the emotions I felt and find some sleep later that night.

We had three runs between 11:30 pm and 6:00 am, none of them severe. With each trip to the ER, a new set of Judy's friends found me and congratulated me. I was expected to fill them in on the details of 'Mom and baby,' and I did my parental duties. About two hours later, when we were relieved by the incoming shift, I was happy to leave to see my wife and daughter.

My daughter. Incredible words, those. *My wife and my daughter.*

Going Home

Two days later, I was at the hospital to bring my family home. I had parked the Camaro as close to the exit we would use as was legally possible, and then I went upstairs to accompany them down. After a series of discharge instructions, Judy took a seat in a wheelchair, and someone handed Amanda to her. Moments later, we were homeward bound.

As the nurse pushing the wheelchair was maneuvering them out of the elevator, I made my way to the parking lot to bring the car front and center. I opened the door on the passenger side and then offered my hand to Judy to help steady her as she stood up. We squared her up, and she made herself comfortable in the Chevy's seat. The nurse handed the baby to her, wished us the best, and went back inside.

I made my way back to the driver's side, found my seatbelt, and fired the engine. My wife and I looked at each other for a moment and smiled. She looked down at Amanda and whispered, "We did it. We are parents. Can you believe this little girl is ours? We did it!" I reached across and touched her arm and took in the sight of my wife and my child. Indeed, we had done it.

I slowly pulled away from the hospital, using more caution than I usually did, and we began our first trip home together. Gone was the freakish heat of two days ago. It was a beautiful, mid-seventies-degree day. All was right in our world.

Reeling In The Years

The next three years sped by like a bunny with wings. Judy returned to work without missing a beat, and Amanda became the base mascot. We didn't take her on any emergency runs or any such thing, but she became quite the little actor for our first aid courses. It was amazing how convincingly Amanda could portray the illness or injuries we gave her to instruct our classes. We told her what to do, and she did it correctly, as she had been taught by the guys at the base.

When she was at the base, the guys would talk to her like she was an adult, and she learned to respond as one. Not that she wasn't your typical little kid; she had all the dolls and toys any girl could have ever wanted. She was one of them when she was with other kids her age. Amanda was just 'one of the guys' when she was at the base.

Mark would read to her, and she was reading to him by the time she turned three. We had another medic from a different base fill in one day. After she schooled him in a game of hers, he told me, "That kid's too darn smart for her own good! She talks better than most adults I know."

Judy and I were quite proud of her. We worked to teach her to learn ahead of her age group and made sure she had plenty of playtime with boys and girls her age. She just seemed to be able to function well at any level she encountered.

We took her to Disney World just before her third birthday. When we met Mickey Mouse in the Kingdom, she walked up to him to say hello. It is well known that the characters in the Kingdom weren't allowed to talk to visitors. By the time I was able to retrieve her, Amanda, or 'Mandi' as I called her, was telling Mickey all about her toys at home and asking him what he would eat for dinner.

As I apologized and picked her up, the gal playing Mickey gave me a smile through the little throat panel that allowed them to breathe when it was hot there in the Florida sun.

The funny thing about her was that 'Daddy' was the only one allowed to call her 'Mandi.' Everyone else, including 'Momma,' had to call her 'Amanda.' She's over forty now, and that's still the deal. I am the only one allowed to call her 'Mandi.' She loved her momma and all the guys, but there was little doubt that she was 'Daddy's Little Girl.'

I asked Judy one night if it bothered her she was taken with me like that. "Never even worried about it, dear. I'm just so happy to be with both of you! I was my 'Daddy's Girl,' so it only fits that things are like they are." Life was good for our little family.

Then came a bitterly cold February night six months later.

It was at or just below zero that night, and Mark and I were hoping we could sleep the night away warm in our beds. Then the phone rang. We were being sent to a fight in the parking lot of a local bar that reportedly had someone severely injured. We had our cold-weather uniforms on, so we were out the door in a matter of a couple of minutes and on the scene three minutes later.

Someone approached Mark, who I could see was bleeding from the face, and I was pointed to a man lying motionless on the pavement of the parking lot. I knelt beside him to inspect him for injuries. Almost immediately, I could tell that he was highly intoxicated. I took my flashlight to examine his face and found that his mouth was a gusher of blood. Someone had used a blunt object and had repeatedly smashed his face with it, knocking out at least seven teeth.

I worked quickly to clear his breathing airway, pulling teeth and blood clots from his mouth so he could breathe. I was about to check the rest of his body for injuries when somewhere behind me, I heard a voice yell my name, telling me to 'look out!' In retrospect, it was that yell that saved my life. I stood up and turned toward the voice, only to see another drunken man holding a shotgun about a dozen steps from me.

He pointed the gun at the man on the pavement, but his alcohol level caused him to falter a bit. His weapon dropped lower just as he pulled its trigger. I saw it flash and then heard it roar. I felt a burning sensation fill my belly and legs. It didn't hurt; it just burned. I can't remember what was said or if I said anything in the immediate aftermath. I just knew something had happened and that my belly burned.

I watched as the man with the gun staggered and fell. Someone ran forward, grabbed the gun, and then landed on him so he couldn't get up again. I walked away from that commotion and headed to where the policeman was interviewing someone who had witnessed the shooting. I was later told that the officer had heard the shot, but when he looked over, the man with the gun was on the ground, and another officer was almost to him.

I didn't remember that part. I just knew that more of my body was burning. As I walked up to the officer, I recalled running my hand inside my uniform jacket. My fingers became slightly sticky. "Officer? Sir?" He turned to look at me. "I'm going over to the ER." The hospital was directly across from the parking lot, and something in me knew I had to get inside. The cop, never realizing that I was injured, told me I should stay there and help treat the wounded.

I was later told that I said to that cop, 'I think I've been shot, sir,' and that I just walked across the street through the ER doors. I remember taking off my heavy uniform jacket and seeing multiple perforations in it as I held it up and then dropped it. I kept walking forward, removing my blue uniform shirt and noting that it also had a lot of tiny holes in it. I held it out, and I could also see a tinge of red against its blue fabric.

I still felt nothing but the burning.

I barely recall much after I removed my white undershirt and dropped it on the floor like a bloody rag. The last thing I remember is looking down at my abdomen and seeing little fountains of blood beginning to roil as I warmed up. The ladies of the ER later told me I was staggering by the time I got to the patient area of the room. Somewhere in a hazy memory, I dreamed about them stripping my clothes off and asking me questions I never answered.

Just as they were about to lift me onto the gurney, they told me I lost consciousness, but not before making one last comment. I allegedly mumbled to the girls that I had worked with for years something like, 'You girls always wanted to see me naked.' I don't deny saying it because I knew I would have said something like that.

I didn't open my eyes for another four days.

By the time they got me to surgery, I had already lost a lot of blood in my abdomen. It had done extensive damage to my intestines, but it had just missed doing damage to my liver and kidneys. I was to be hospitalized for a couple of weeks as the possibility of infection was quite high. I was in pain, but I knew well that I could have quickly bled out from that type of injury.

During the second week of my recovery, Judy and Mandi visited me. We were having a good time considering the situation, and Judy was telling me about some antics our daughter had pulled in the kitchen. In the middle of the laughter, my surgeon walked in and told me about my last blood work results.

He told me my white blood cell count was running just a bit higher than usual, which was good considering all that had happened. He also told me that as long as I didn't have a flare-up of infection, I could go home in four to five days. Judy and I were glad to hear that news, and I felt her squeeze my hand. "You came very close to death, Mr. Greenhoe. You are one lucky man."

He was about to leave when Mandi approached him and tugged on his white coat. He knelt to her level and asked if she had a question. Just as serious as you please, she told the doctor, "God wouldn't let my daddy die because He knows I need him." A profound statement from a little girl only three and a half years old, and it was obvious it had moved the doctor.

"You are right, little one. You need your daddy, and I'm glad to tell you he will be home with you and your momma soon. We are taking good care of him so he can get back to you as soon as he can." She reached out and shook the man's hand. Her serious, big blue eyes stared at him as she thanked him. I am sure she had made him uneasy because he was out the door at an unusually fast pace.

Neither Judy nor I said anything for a few minutes. We had always been astounded by our little girl's wisdom, but her words seemed to unnerve many people. As we held hands and whispered back and forth, Amanda was happily playing with some plastic animals she had brought in with her play purse.

About an hour later, one of the nurses came in to do a dressing change, and Judy used that as her excuse to go home. Her sister visited us for a while. She was a great help, serving as a babysitter until I was out of the hospital. I hugged and kissed my daughter and then my wife, and as they walked out the door, I told them both that I loved them.

Four days later, I was released with strict instructions not to lift anything that weighed over five pounds. They also gave me some prescriptions to prevent any infection that might still be hidden somewhere. On the way home, Judy drove me over to the ambulance base, where the crew gave me a big welcome home card and a small cake. We talked for a bit, but the recovery period had left me much weaker than I had thought possible, and she took me home to my bed.

We sat on the couch for a while. Judy snuggled in beside me, and Amanda balanced on my knee. She chattered on and on about a new doll someone had given her, pointing out that the toy had blonde hair, just like she had. It was good to be home.

When we finally retired for the night, I climbed in first, followed by the baby and then Judy. Amanda held one of my hands and one of Judy's and talked about how much she was glad that we were a family again. I never knew where she had gotten the concept of the family so young. She became an amazing woman and mother in her own right.

The next four days were as if we had picked up right from the day before my shooting. Then came the telephone call at 3 am. The hospital supervisor asked me to come in to pick up Judy from work. When I asked if she was sick, the woman told me, "I think she has had a nervous breakdown."

I got up and dressed within three minutes and then woke Amanda, who was still in her pajamas. She wasn't happy about getting out of bed until I told her we would pick up Momma. She loved going to visit the hospital, and the thought of bringing Momma home made it that much better.

It was now the early weeks of March, and while the nighttime temps were no longer hovering near zero, it was still cold. I had the baby sitting on the couch while I went out and started the car to warm it up. Once I came back in, I talked her into walking out with me instead of being carried due to my shooting injuries. I had found the trick was making her think it was her choice to walk, not mine.

By the time we were in the car and belted in, the interior was warming up, and we were on our way. The hospital was only nine miles away, and there was no traffic, allowing us to get there in about ten minutes. I unbuckled the baby and got her to walk in beside me, where the supervisor met me.

On our way to the room where they had taken Judy, I asked what had set her off. It had never occurred to me she was having a problem with anything. "Apparently, someone asked her how you were doing, and she began to talk about how bad your injury was, and she just froze up and began to cry. Once she started, we couldn't get her to stop."

As we went to the nurse's station, I recognized one of the girls there, so I asked if she could entertain my little one until I got things under control. I had no idea what I was going to find, and the last thing I wanted was for Amanda to see her momma crying. Someone pulled out a coloring book and some crayons from under the desk, and soon, my baby was busy at the desk coloring a lake and forest scene.

I was led down a long hallway. Once at the end of the hall, we were shown the door to the room where Judy was sitting. I asked to be allowed to go in by myself, and the supervisor backed away. I knocked gently on the door and walked in to find my wife sitting in a mostly darkened room, her head in her hands, softly sobbing.

I stood next to her and whispered, "Babe? What's wrong?" She hadn't realized I was there, but she stood up and flung herself at me once she saw me. As she hugged me, I felt a slight twinge in my belly, but nothing that was going to hurt anything. "What's wrong, Judy? Please tell me?"

I waited for her to respond by just holding her and stroking her face softly. I knew that pushing her for answers would not get me away. We stood together, softly swaying a silent dance for nearly ten minutes before she spoke. "I just realized that you could have died. You could have died! I couldn't live without you. I'm not strong enough. I couldn't take care of our daughter on my own."

Over the years, I have found that everyone has a tipping point. Some people reach it quickly, and some people can be pushed a long way before they tip over emotionally. Judy was not a weak woman. She had forced herself to get through the time when she had to be strong for the baby and me. Now that I had resumed control of events in our life, she no longer had to be strong anymore. When she was asked by someone else about the danger I was in the night I was shot, her strength had left her.

I couldn't just tell her that 'it's alright' because she knew I was still under strict medical supervision. So I reminded her that when I could not shoulder my responsibilities, she had stood up and handled both jobs of running the family and working full time. In a time of uncertainty, she had stood tall, done her job, and cared for Amanda and me. "And you did a darn good job, dear. You did an excellent job of caring for the baby and me. You are a strong woman. You are."

I held her close and continued to whisper to her. "I'm proud of you. I'm very proud of you. I want you to know something. I was going to wait a bit longer to be sure it was what I wanted to do, but I know what I'm going to do now. Can we sit down and talk about this?" I was doing my best to gently guide her to the present and how we would deal with it.

It took another minute, but Judy finally sat down with me on the bed in the room. She was holding my hand, and I could see the tears streaming down her face. "Judy, calm down for me, please?" I saw her gently nod her head.

"The second day I was home, a lawyer for the county stopped over while you were sleeping. I don't think they want me to continue as a medic anymore. They know it will take a lot of physical therapy to get me ready to go back to work." Judy was looking me in my eyes for the first time since I arrived.

"They've made me an offer to retire at sixty percent of my normal wages, and we would still keep our health insurance for eighteen months. They would continue to cover all of my work-related healthcare issues. I could be here with Amanda, be here for you, and get paid to be a husband and a father. There would be no more family disputes, no more bar fights, and no more running out of here on icy and snow-covered roads. I'd be home every night." Judy gripped my hands even tighter.

"Unless you tell me otherwise, I will give them my answer tomorrow morning. I would have to finish my paperwork at the base office and then sign the legal papers. Of course, I'd have our lawyer look everything over to make sure there is no legal loophole for them. As soon as he gives me the okay, I'll sign them. You wouldn't have to worry about me being shot again or anything else like that. Is that alright with you?"

Once again, Judy nearly leaped on me as she grabbed me to hold me closer. "Please, just sign the papers and get away from this business. Please, do it for the baby and me!" I didn't want to quit working as a medic.

I loved the work and the adventures I had had, but I cared more for my wife and my daughter. I promised her that the moment our lawyer gave me the go-ahead, I would sign the agreement to leave my job.

A light knock on the door was followed by Mandi walking into the room to join us. The nurse whispered that she couldn't persuade her to stay at the desk any longer. My ladies were like that. I smiled and told her it was alright. "What's wrong, Momma? Why are you crying? Daddy, what's wrong with Momma?"

I helped her to sit between Judy and me and told her, "Momma was scared that I was hurting after that man did that nasty thing to me. I told Momma that I was just fine, but she didn't believe me. Can you tell her that Daddy is alright?"

Our daughter stood on the bed and hugged her mother. "It's alright, Momma; Daddy isn't hurt anymore. The doctors fixed him. Don't cry, Momma. Don't cry. Let me kiss you, Momma. It will make you feel better." Amanda leaned over and softly kissed Judy's face in several places. "It's alright, Momma. Daddy and I are here. Can we go home, Daddy? Can we take Momma home now?"

"Yes, Baby Girl, we can take Momma home now. She was just scared, but she will be alright now. Won't you, Momma?" Judy sobbed as she hugged the three-year-old adult who stood between us. Amanda climbed down from the bed and took Judy's hand.

"Come on, Momma, let's go home." I put my hand out to help her stand. I found a cloth and wiped her face clean, kissing her as often as I could. We walked out the door and down the hall. Judy couldn't look at her co-workers, but Amanda looked over her shoulder as we walked away. "My Momma isn't feeling well, so we are going to take her home. Good night." With that, we were headed home.

Judy wasn't able to work for a week. I spoke with her supervisor (who, in truth, was a friend of ours), and I explained to her I thought Judy had 'hit a wall' of pent-up emotions following my injuries. She could have gone back several days sooner, but she had a lot of vacation days built up. The hospital supervisor was kind enough to allow her to take them on short notice.

On her second day after 'the incident,' as we came to call it, Judy and Mandi went with me to visit our lawyer to discuss the buy-out the ambulance service was offering me. I had gone through it at least a dozen times and found nothing I thought might be detrimental to me later, but I wasn't a lawyer. I had dropped a copy off at his office the day before to help speed things up.

When we were led back to Mr. Dunne's office, we exchanged niceties briefly. He had met Judy before, but he hadn't seen our daughter. Amanda was good at meeting people, and it broke me up when adults were given an extended little hand to shake, followed by her telling them, "I'm happy to meet you!"

He made the mistake of calling her 'Mandi,' and the attorney was promptly informed her name was 'Amanda.' I told him, "Sorry; everyone but Daddy calls her Amanda. Daddy gets to call her 'Mandi' or our newest one, 'Baby Girl.' It's a thing between us." The man smiled and took his seat behind a large cherry wood desk.

Mr. Dunne rifled through some papers, finally locating the one he wanted and handing it to me. "If you are intent on leaving, this is a good deal for you. They maintain your health insurance plan just as you have it now. They continue to be responsible for your current medical situation in full for 180 days and then at 75% up to and through the next five years."

He pointed out the wording to Judy and, of course, Amanda. "They also agree to pay you 65% of your base pay for 180 days. Note that I've added that the countdown on all of this begins the day you sign this agreement." I nodded my agreement as he continued.

"There are a couple of minor things I've changed here. They may or may not go for these changes, but you're ahead of the game if they do. If they don't, you've lost nothing you didn't have before."

Judy asked him a couple of questions, and then, based on his answers, I asked two follow-up questions. Just before we were going to leave, he told me he had to ask me a couple of questions. I sat back down and waited. "This may be too personal, but I have to ask. Why are you taking this buyout? I've seen the injury reports, and I see no reason you won't have a full recovery. Why are you leaving?"

I don't know why, but I put my hands together and looked at my shoes for a few moments. I suppose it was to gather my emotions, but I know I sighed as I searched for the right way to respond. "Mr. Dunne, I don't want to quit, but I have to ask you: do you have something that you really would do anything to keep?"

He looked at me strangely and told me he thought the century-old piano his grandmother had given him would probably be high on that list. He thought a moment longer and added a couple of other objects.

I was looking at my feet again as I talked to him. "With all due respect to your grandmother and her piano, I think my reasons are two. I don't want to leave my job. I love my job, but I love my wife and daughter more than anything else. We don't get credit for it, but we put our lives in danger every time we leave that parking barn in that ambulance. Discounting the various minor injuries I have incurred, this makes the second time I have been shot."

I don't think he had realized that I had been shot before. It hadn't been an intentional shooting, but shot is shot. "I've been stabbed once, right here in the chest. Had it not been for me moving a notepad at the very last second, his knife would have gone deep into my chest and probably my heart. I have the scar to prove it."

Judy began to get upset that I might say something to hurt my working relationship with the attorney, but I was ready to leave when he asked me a question. Now, he was getting his answer. "I knew this was a dangerous job when I took it. I was single then. Now I have a wife, a kind and sweet woman. A woman who is better than I ever deserve. She has blessed me with a beautiful daughter. I'm leaving out of love for them. I have a degree and can get a job when I want one. I can't take a chance to be taken out by a nut-job and leave these two ladies alone."

Mr. Dunne studied me for a moment, smiled, and nodded. "I understand. Too many people don't realize when they've got it good. You aren't one of those people. I'm happy for you and your family. I wish you nothing but happiness."

He stood up at the same time that I did and shook my hand. Mandi climbed down from her chair and stood beside me. Her baby-sized hand reached up to meet Mr. Dunne's hand, and she gave it a firm handshake. Her voice was crystal clear as she wished him a good day. I saw him smile, and he opened the door for us.

As we walked out, he called out to his secretary. She walked partially down the hallway, but he met her partway. "No charge for the Greenhoe family for this meeting." He patted me on the back and returned to his office. Maybe it was out of kindness. Perhaps it was because my daughter had made him smile. I want to think it was because, for a moment in his life, he realized that not everything revolved around money. I never found out.

From there, I took my papers to the supervisor of the entire ambulance company. I showed him the additions Mr. Dunne had suggested. He looked them over and told me he would have those changes added to his copy, and I could come back the next day and sign them.

We started out of the door, but I turned around. "You need to know that I loved this job and the people we treated. If I were a single man, I'd return in a few months. But with everything that has happened in the past two years, it's time to call it a game. I just wanted you to know that." He smiled and told me I would be missed.

One last handshake later, and we were all in the Camaro and on our way home.

A Knock On The Door

The next ten months brought Judy back to her usual self-confidence at work while being an ever-loving mother and wife. We had found a new house on the edge of a small town. It was quiet, with a large backyard and a large wooded area behind it. It needed some work, but we were young and began to restore it.

Within a month, we replaced the entire kitchen and installed new paneling and carpeting in the living room and all three bedrooms. The final touch was a complete rebuild of everything in the bathroom. After two months, a bunch of friends helped us replace the roof, basically giving us a new home. Life was good.

Amanda continued to thrive, leaving that baby stage behind her as she became a child. Her vocabulary astounded most adults. We never spoke 'baby talk' to her, and because Judy and I were avid readers, she learned the love of books. She always had her own opinion about things, and anyone who engaged her in conversation was going to hear it. She would often 'argue' with an adult and win. As the years went on, that was a trait that only got stronger.

I used my time to get my nursing education, much to the chagrin of some of my instructors. Many of the things they were teaching weren't what I had seen and learned as a paramedic. I challenged one particular instructor several times, and she became furious with me. I was almost tossed out of the program, and I knew it, so I got permission for an ER doctor I knew quite well to stop by our nursing class and explain why I was right, and she wasn't.

I wasn't trying to intimidate the instructor, but what use is learning things that weren't right? Remembering the time frame in which this happened, the medical profession was rapidly changing. My medical training was newer than hers, and our learning came from top physicians in the emergency medical field. It didn't make me really popular with the instructor, but my classmates got a better education.

I finished the courses and then came the waiting period to take the state exam to get a nursing license. Our timing had been terrible, as we had just missed a state-wide test, and we had to wait for the next one to roll around. In the meantime, I had been offered a job as a medical technician in a local prison. The pay was much better than I had ever made, so I took the job.

This job became the background for some of my books, all based on incidents or people I met in prison. I talked with men lodged in the psych wards of a cluster of six prisons. Some men fit into prison life quite quickly, and others never could. My job was to draw them out into the prison society.

I had taken some courses in psychology, and while I never got a degree in that field, it at least gave me something that allowed me to work with the men I found there. My job was to talk with the guys who had hidden in their cells, thus avoiding social contact with nearly everyone. Isolation isn't good for anyone, and an already disturbed individual becomes a danger to everyone when he locks himself away.

I remember the warden telling me when I hired in, 'I hire nine guys to be muscle, and one guy to be brains. I see you haven't been to the gym for a while. Do you understand why I hired you?' I did. We took three weeks of training to learn how the prison worked 'inside.' and what was allowable and what was not.

Walking into prison the first few times can be an intimidating thing for even the hardest of criminals, and for someone who has never seen the inside of a jail, let alone prison, it could be terrifying. While I wasn't as scared as most of my prison employee classmates, it would be a total fib if I were to tell you that I wasn't afraid. It was at least a month before I developed the mental toughness required so that the slamming of the steel barred doors didn't send a bolt of lightning surging through me.

The first and foremost problem was the constant noise level. If the birds chirping outside annoy you, you should stay away from prison. Even at night, a steady roar of voices is in the air. A steady stream of vulgarities was available in every corner of the place.

The intimidation level was another problem. While almost every guy in there would tell you that they were innocent, most of them hadn't gotten there because they lifted a couple of dollars out of the church offering plate. They had been intimidating people in life on the outside, and the only way you could survive was to try to be more intimidating than the guy in front of you. Fights were always breaking out, and I saw a lot of guys roughed up to the point that they were in a real hospital for a few days.

After a few days inside, I started working with one of the prison psychologists, and we fit together well. He explained what he wanted me to do and the best way to do it. I was free to streamline his technique to fit my style. Shortly, I was given a list of men that someone in the prison system had decided were becoming a danger to themselves or others by becoming recluses.

I was to approach them and attempt to get them to talk to me. I was given an extensive background sheet on each man, so I had a frame of reference for his crimes, prison behavioral problems in the past, and other information the prison psychologist thought pertinent.

From there, I was to break through to them and get them to talk about anything. The goal was being achieved as long as they began to speak again. I told the psychologist that my dad had always told me I could get a watermelon to talk to me, and he said to me that I would need every bit of that ability to speak with these guys.

The first guy I was assigned may have been a fluke, or maybe I just got lucky. Within two hours, I had him answer a few questions for me. I had been part of a debate team, and I had learned that you could encourage someone to talk or shut it down based on the questions you asked. Within a week, the guy was out walking around with the rest of the men in that particular ward. The doctor was pleased with that result.

My next assigned man was a much different case. I spent a lot of time talking to him, but he never so much as looked at me. I can't remember exactly how long it took, but it had to have been two weeks of me talking to myself with him in the room. I was telling him a story about something I had done while camping when he broke in and corrected my facts. I was shocked to hear him speak.

One of the more significant rules in talking with these guys was never giving out personal information. If you had ever spoken with some of the guys I met, you'd know why that rule was needed. I was describing the side trip that Judy and I had taken to Mt. Rushmore. I had given him the presidents on the monument, with the preface of, 'From left to right, you have…' at which point I accidentally switched the names of Lincoln and Roosevelt around.

I knew better because Roosevelt's face was sunk much deeper into the mountain than Lincoln's due to an accident in the carving. Judy and I had talked about that a lot during our drive following that visit. I said no more than, "There's Washington, Jefferson, Lincoln, and Roosevelt…" when he cursed at me. He told me that it was Roosevelt and Lincoln unless someone switched them.

I looked at him a moment, then picked up just like we had been having a civil conversation. "You're right, of course. When you were there, had they started that other monument dedicated to Crazy Horse yet?" He cursed again and told me that they had started that one years before he had been there and that there was a fat chance it was ever going to be finished. Now, we had a common point of reference.

Over the next ten days, I was able to drag a few more words out of him every day. I doubted that he had ever been much of a conversationalist, but he was talking again. I would make a statement with a small error of fact in it, and he would curse at me, call me stupid, and correct me. When I was reporting to the doctor on this guy, he told me that sometimes progress could be measured by the word with some guys.

Over the next year or so, I was to work with a lot of men. I was able to get most of them talking but had three guys that never acknowledged I was in the room. On the other hand, I met some men who weren't the kind of guys you would want to meet on their terms. Once they began to talk, they would regale me with the stories of how they killed people who had done nothing more than be in the wrong place at the wrong time. While it was often terrifying, it was always fascinating to me.

Then, there came a day when I should have listened to my instincts and stayed home. I had a forty-five-minute drive to work, and every mile of that trip, something in my brain kept telling me I needed to stop, call in sick, and go home. I didn't listen, and it cost me at least five years of my life. (I wrote a book about that ordeal entitled "My Long Road Back" if the problems of closed head injuries are of interest to you.)

When I got to work, nothing was as it should have been. Except for one lone individual, everyone else was still locked down. When I asked what was going on, I was told that the man wandering the dayroom was hallucinating, and no one could get him to go to his 'house,' as prison cells are called. They had notified the incoming security team but the team hadn't had time to get there yet.

I looked out the office window and saw a man I had worked with for a while. I asked to be allowed to talk with him. As I stepped out into the room with him, he recognized me and warmly greeted me. I asked him what was happening to him just then, and he began to explain. He had been watching television the night before, and the President had broken into his local programming to announce that he had pardoned him, effective immediately.

I asked him to sit down with me to discuss the matter. He walked over to one of the room tables and even pulled out a chair for me. He went over the details again, and I listened as attentively as possible. When he was finished explaining, I asked him, "Do you trust me?" He told me that I was one of the few officers in the prison that he did trust. I thanked him and continued. "If I promise you that I will check into this and get it straight, would you go back to your house and take your medicines?" He promised that he would do that for me.

I stood up, and he followed me down the hall to where his quarters were situated. He walked in and sat on his bed. I told him that I would be right back with his medicines. The office nurse rarely, if ever, stepped out into the dayroom, and she never went to the house of a prisoner, but she followed me down and handed me his medications. He then took them. I thanked him and locked his door.

If the story had ended there, everything would have been just fine. His meds would have kicked in, and in an hour or so, he would have become himself again, and all would have been well. That didn't happen.

The nurse had told the prison doctor about the incident and set up a meeting. I was assigned to go see the doctor as the prisoner's escort, and I knew right away that this wasn't going to end well.

The doctor was from the Philippines and was not the best English speaker, especially English spoken by black men. The doctor asked him what was happening, and when the prisoner tried to explain, he brushed him off rather rudely. Without any warning, the man exploded and leaped forward to beat the doctor for his crass words.

My partner and I did our best to stop him, taking severe blows from his massive fists while the doctor hid under his big oak desk. Somewhere along the line, my partner had been thrown through the office window.

During the scuffle, I caught an elbow directly to the nose, sending bolts of pain and bright lights through my head. I was later told that I was holding my nose with one hand and pawing at the air with the other.

I don't know why I was doing that, but apparently, it provoked the man who, just twenty minutes earlier, had pulled out a chair for me, and he grabbed me by the head. When I saw the video several months later, it was almost like a cartoon. He grabbed the top of my head and began to hit me on the side of my face six or seven times. This man had monstrous-sized fists, and I don't recall much of anything until help came pouring in to secure the scene.

I stumbled around the room until I found something to lean against to support myself. Once there, I braced myself in an attempt to recover my senses. I felt something warm and sticky in my hands that I initially took as blood. It was cerebral spinal fluid, and there was lots of it dripping into my hands. As a medic, I knew that I was in serious trouble.

I won't bore you with the details of this incident here, but the next thing that I seriously remember is when I woke up in a hospital some fifty miles away four days later. I remember hearing Judy's voice asking someone what my prognosis was. The other voice, which I later found to be the neurosurgeon who had admitted me, told her that it depended on whether I developed a brain infection from the leaking spinal fluid. I fell asleep again and didn't wake up for another couple of days.

I got lucky in that, other than a headache that lasted the next four years and some behavioral issues due to the soon-to-be-discovered 'closed head injury' syndrome, I walked away from it unmarked. I had suffered a cribriform plate fracture, the small, thin bone just above the nose area in the base of the skull. When it fractured, it allowed spinal fluid to pour out my nose and down my throat. It slowly became a steady drip and then sealed itself. It could have been much worse.

While I floundered about for the first year, Judy maintained the home, our daughter, and her job like the trooper she had always been when the pressure was on her. She never took a sick day nor missed either a preschool event for Amanda or a holiday dinner.

Due to my closed head injuries (CHI), there were a lot of things that I missed, but Judy and the little one were always where they should have been. It was nearly ten years later when the aftereffects of CHI were discovered. In the meantime, everyone else thought I was 'faking' it.

Somewhere as I was emerging from the fog of that injury, Judy became pregnant with our second child two years later. The strange thing is that, while I had forgotten so much of that period, I remember the night that it happened. It was a Valentine's Day evening, and I was more 'normal' than I had been in a while.

As I look back, I know that she was hoping that every time I became lucid, I would remain that way so she could step away from the harness. As strong as she was at work, she didn't like being the family's decision-maker. If I could go back in time and change just one thing in my life, I would go back to that morning when I was injured. I should have paid better attention to the screaming in my head to call in, and gone home.

Judy had never been happy with my decision to work in the prison. It was good money, but she knew it was fraught with danger. It was the first of four situations in our lives that led to her emotional and then physical breakdown.

As her delivery date grew closer, I became more aware of what I was doing. Judy willingly allowed me to step back into the lead harness. In retrospect, it was much too soon, but she wanted to be free of that position, so she stepped back from it, content to follow me. I had some good, some excellent, and some bad days, but I was nowhere near ready to 'lead' the family, something Judy would soon learn.

Just as Judy's first pregnancy went well, her second time around was almost textbook. I was having a great day when our son was born, and Dr. Adams allowed me to deliver our son. I knew that this doctor was aware of my situation, so she was ready to have me step aside should I fail to respond appropriately. Thankfully, everything went perfectly.

Our son, named after my Father and me, came into the world at noon on a November day. He tipped in at twenty-one inches long and eight pounds, twelve ounces. My Aunt Phyllis was one of our first visitors, and her remark gave him the nickname he would carry all of his life. She looked at him as he was nursing and told me, "That's a big name for such a little guy. If he were mine, I'd call him 'Skip.'"

From that day forward, that was his name. Twenty-some years later, he would meet a President as he serviced Air Force One in his capacity with the US Air Force. When that service was finished, he met personally with the President, who had asked to meet him. When asked his name, he rattled off his military rank and title. When asked what his family called him, my son replied, 'Skip.' He would meet the man three more times, and each time, the President of the United States would talk with him; he called him 'Skip.' Just one of those funny little things that happen in life.

We went home with our son and daughter, very happy and proud. Our lives seemed to have found their feet again, and all was well, at least for a month. I still hadn't been able to work after my head injury, but I was beginning to think clearly again. For that reason, I was there when Judy fell while holding Skip, but I had no idea what caused it. She stood up, took about two steps, and then went down like a sack of potatoes.

I ran to them and found that she was awake but not alert. Somehow, the baby had come down in a full laundry basket, and while he was crying, he was unhurt. I turned my attention to Judy and found that she was slowly becoming aware of what had happened. She began to cry that she had hurt Skip, and I assured her that he was alright. I managed to get her into the car and took them to the Emergency Room.

The doctor there ran multiple blood tests and neurological exams on her, only to find that the sole deviancy was that her blood sugar was just under normal levels. It had never been low before, and there would never be a time it would read low again, but that one time, it was low. The doctor told me that it was the most likely cause of her fall. Skip was examined and found to be uninjured.

We went home, and I tucked Judy into bed and took care of the children. Judy woke up feeling much better the next morning, although still quite ashamed of almost hurting Skip. It took a lot of talking, but I showed her the papers on her blood tests. She looked them over and finally accepted the fact that she had passed out due to low blood sugar. Then, there came a knock on the door.

I opened the door to find a 'social services worker' there, demanding entrance and the ability to inspect the baby. I told her that she could 'demand' all she wanted, but she could go fly a kite unless she had court papers. I had seen this little game play out far too many times during my EMS career, and I was not about to allow those people into my life.

Social workers have their place, but I have seen good homes broken and children taken because some do-gooder made a 'decision.' If we had had a history of child abuse or neglect, I could understand it, but we took pride in how our children were being raised. Of course, there were further repercussions, but they were all met and rebuffed. Our lawyer stepped in, and it all went away. Well, most of it went away.

The thought that a social worker had even questioned her about abusing her child started Judy off on a tangent. It didn't take long, and it caused her to lose her confidence again. It took me a good seven weeks to get her head straight back. It also set the stage for the next event that was only four months away.

I'm Sorry

Things had calmed down, and Judy returned to work after her mandatory eight-week maternity leave and the additional four-week vacation request I had requested for her. Our romance had returned to its original vigor, and even the kids enjoyed sitting together and holding hands.

Amanda loved the bedtime routine of hugging, kissing, and saying, 'I love you.' Despite her initial dislike of having a baby brother, she had become quite protective of him. Thanksgiving and Christmas get-togethers were happily attended, and we rang in the New Year with hopes of a return to a healthy life.

On the sixth of January, Judy and I were sitting on the couch, talking about what we hoped to achieve in the next year. She acted like the girl I had met and romanced just seven years before, and I was in love again. One more time in our lives, there was a knock on the door.

Judy had gone into the kitchen to put some dishes in the sink while I answered the door. As I swung it open, a massive shadow of a man filled the entrance. It was a Michigan State trooper. He had a piece of paper and asked if I was the person on that paper. I told him I was. "I'm sorry to tell you this, but this is an eviction notice from the State of Michigan."

He handed me the papers, and I read the words. It was filled with all kinds of legal jargon, and I looked at him for an explanation. "Well, sir, unfortunately, you aren't the only one I've visited today. It seems that some twenty years ago, several homes in this area were lost by their original owners due to a failure to pay property taxes. This should have been handled then, but they fell through the cracks."

I was speechless. The officer continued to talk, and I attempted to understand what was happening. I showed him the title of the house and the pages where I had paid the taxes. He shook his head in a visible show of empathy and continued with his bad news.

"Sir, I've spoken with three others in town who have told me the same thing. All I know is that somehow, back in the mid-1950s, your home defaulted to the State of Michigan for failure to pay the property taxes. It went unnoticed until last fall when someone found the error, which is why I am here today. You have ten days to evacuate the premises, or you and your personal property will be forcibly removed. I am extremely sorry."

I hadn't noticed that Judy had returned to the room until I heard her faint behind me. The officer helped me get her to the couch and asked if he should call for an ambulance. I thanked him but declined his offer. He apologized one more time, leaving me with my wife and the bundle of papers. The man had been polite during his visit, and while my mind was in turmoil, I was thankful for his understanding of our situation and how he handled it.

I closed the door behind him and went to sit with Judy, who was sobbing away on the couch. I assured her that there had to be a mistake and that I would visit our attorney and get this handled. I was wrong. I went to the lawyer's office, all my papers in hand, thoroughly expecting him to tell me the steps we would need to take to correct the problem. He got on his phone and made four calls to various people. When he hung up, he told me that there was no remedy for the problem.

Apparently, the state had run one of those ads you see in the classifieds of local newspapers warning that the 'current occupants' of the following addresses had sixty days to pay these back taxes plus the interest owed. I had never read any of those notices, and neither had five others in our town. We had to move within the next ten days. The lawyer told me I could not remove anything by law. If it had been nailed, screwed, or otherwise 'attached' to the house, it had to stay.

On the seventh of January, it was five above, with a significant snowstorm moving in. I had to pack all our belongings in the back of the car and the beds of pickups three of my friends brought. We ended up moving in with my father. I also had to deal with a hysterical wife and daughter.

We left behind over ten thousand dollars of improvements, a lot of money back then. I had hoped that the house would be put up for auction so we could attempt to recover it. Ultimately, our home and all the other five homes were bulldozed. No one gave a damn about the contents inside. It devastated my wife even further. There was no reason that the state would not have given us a chance to redeem our home.

The lot our home stood on would sit vacant and empty for another fifteen years. Every time we drove by it, I would hear my wife cry. One more time, I spent months reining her emotions back into check. It was difficult, especially when I was doing my best not to cry with her.

Everything we had built went down in a pile of rubble for a missed payment of a seventy-eight dollar tax bill, one that had been missed by someone who had died twelve years before we bought it. It caused the second major collapse of my wife, setting the stage for the last two.

A Return To Normal

Over the next fourteen years, our lives remained trouble-free, and thus, things became routine. Judy had regained her emotional footing and was doing very well at work. She became the department supervisor. Part of her job was to rewrite and update department policies and procedures to meet the new standards and policies that both state and national agencies placed on obstetrical units. She also won several 'Nurse of the Year' awards for her work.

Our children were doing well in school. I was now a nurse working in the local emergency room, and we had found a new home. Now and again, I could see Judy take a deep sigh as we passed the empty lot where our other house had stood, but she never brought it up again. It was still an emotional scar for her, but I had convinced her you couldn't waste time and energy worrying about things you can't control. I know it took a lot of work for her to remain quiet, but she did.

The first big test of her emotional stability came the day my father died. We were supposed to have been at his place about the time he fell victim to a heart attack, but we had gone for a walk in a nearby wood. A fallen tree out by this small lake made for an excellent bench. We took advantage of what was a beautiful June day to watch the animals that made the lake their home.

I looked at my watch and realized we were almost an hour late, so we returned to the house. I had only walked through the door when the phone rang. When I answered it, all I heard was my mother screaming for me to get over there because my father had 'collapsed.' We flew over to his home, only to find that an ambulance had taken him to the ER in town.

Coincidently, just a week prior, Dad had spoken to me about being his medical caretaker in the event he became ill. He told me he didn't want to lie around in a coma forever, saying that if he 'looked like a vegetable, plant me like one.' Dad was famous for his farmer's sayings. I went to the local hospital and walked into the room where they were doing CPR on my dad.

One look at the EKG machine, and I knew they were going through their paces and nothing more. I asked the ER physician to stop the code, and initially, he refused. Fortunately, the ER nurse on duty had been a friend of mine from my EMS days, and he intervened on my behalf. The doctor asked me why I would want to stop the code, and I asked him, "Have you ever successfully revived anyone running that heart rhythm?" He had not.

"I spoke to Dad only a week ago, and he asked me to stop this valiant in this type of wasted effort. Please stop the code." It took a moment, but the medical team stopped doing compressions. I watched the monitor as the tender, loving heart my father always had worn on his sleeve ground to a halt. I was doing my best to control myself as I walked out the door.

My oldest sister didn't understand what I had done, but she knew I was the one who asked the doctor to stop treating him. She cursed at me and tried to slap me, but she missed. I just told her I was sorry and that I was doing what Dad had asked me to do. She was upset, but I understood. It was about three years before she would speak to me civilly again. I never pressed the issue because I had seen this scenario play out in ERs most of my life. It was never easy to do the right thing.

I left the emergency room area and walked to my car. I knew there was nothing more I could do there. I was met there by my daughter and my wife. Neither of them had gone inside, and I had to tell them what had happened. I got big hugs from both of them, and we got into the car and went home.

I fully understood that Judy had had an extremely close relationship with my father, and I was concerned about how it would affect her. While she had done some crying in the time leading up to the funeral, she held up much better than I had expected. We also had attended a luncheon that the local VFW held for our family and friends, but Judy held strong.

When we arrived back home, I took a shower, and after a moment, I felt her slip into the shower with me. We held each other close for several minutes, both of us crying. We were able to cry there merely because the water washed our tears away. While I wasn't ashamed of my tears, we realized our children were watching and learning from what we were doing.

We had both witnessed the hysterics of some families and thought our children needed to learn about the process. While sadness and tears were expected for a time, part of living was dying. We sat with the kids and talked about our feelings and emotions. I told them the reason behind the lunch they had held after the funeral was to remind people that while it was all right to be sad, they had to continue to live. Eating in a community setting helps the family begin their lives again.

We listened to their questions and thoughts about the last three days. Both of them had issues, and Judy and I did our best to give them answers that would make sense and help them regain their emotional feet again. I told them there was no shame in what they were feeling and that everyone had the same feelings sweeping over them.

Judy also explained that every family did things differently, explaining that, as they got older, they could develop their own beliefs and practices for their own lives. She stressed to them we would always be there to answer any questions they might have over the upcoming months. She then gave them their little phrase to signal that they needed a moment to talk.

Our house was quiet that night. After the kids were in their rooms, I heard crying from both bedrooms. As the next couple of weeks passed, I spoke with both of them when they asked for a moment of my time. They both sought us out for hugs to help them work through their feelings.

Gradually, they both came to terms with their grandfather's passing. Two months later, on his birthday, our son told a story about something Grandpa had done that had made him laugh. Our daughter remembered her own story, and she told me about it. When the day was over, I knew more tears had been spilled, but laughter was slowly finding its way back into their lives. It was an essential step in life.

As we went to bed that night, Judy and I lay in our bed. We held hands in the dark as we always had, and I asked her how she was holding up. I heard a small sniffle, but in a clear voice, she told me she missed 'Dad' with every bone in her body. She explained she was glad that he had gone suddenly, with little to no pain. Not everyone would leave their family so easily.

While that sounds cruel to some, both of us had seen people hang on for weeks with drugs and IV fluids running non-stop. We had witnessed families standing around the bed, some crying, some plotting, and some fighting. The hospital bill would drain whatever family resources might be left behind, dividing the family and leaving everyone upset. She thought that Dad would have appreciated the way that he had left us, and I agreed. We kissed, said 'I love you' to one another, and fell asleep.

There Was Blood All Over

I watched Judy for a delayed response to my father's death, but nothing happened. In fact, over the next five years, she only had one 'bad spell.' Our daughter was out of high school, and our son was a junior. Everything had been going along as best as anyone's life could be until I noticed a change in her. At first, I couldn't identify the problem, but a day later, she talked to someone I couldn't see. The person wasn't hidden. She wasn't there.

I listened more attentively and realized that she was also 'word-salading,' a phenomenon where the person puts random words together that typically would not be together. I was familiar with the situation, but I wasn't aware just then that it was an early sign of dementia and schizophrenia.

When it didn't stop, I took her to her doctor and explained what was going on. I reminded him of Judy's past and that her mom had slipped into dementia, Alzheimer's, and Parkinson's disease. He listened to me and talked with Judy, but I wasn't wholly convinced that she knew it. He asked me if I could help her get a urine specimen, which I did.

Her urine was slightly cloudy and had a distinct odor to it, and sure enough, it came back positive for a urinary tract infection. Judy had had the occasional UTI, but precious few for a woman her age. As he was writing her a prescription, he told me that while it wasn't common, some women have diminished mental capacities when they develop a UTI. I had worked in an ER for a long time and had seen a ton of women with UTIs, but I had never witnessed a case like this.

I took her home, had our son watch her, and fetched her antibiotics from a local pharmacy. When I returned, I gave her a dose and another before she went to bed. During the night, I locked all the doors in case she might hazard a trip outside without waking me.

The next morning, Judy was nothing like she had been just twenty-four hours before. Her speech was normal, and she knew who I was and appeared normal in every way. She had no particular recollection of visiting the doctor, but she knew by the prescription bottle that she must have been somewhere. I added that little piece of information about the UTIs to my brain, but I still wasn't confident that was the precise thing that had set her off.

A few months later, Judy decided she wanted a new living room set up and learned that her former employer needed a short-time fill-in nurse in OB. She asked if I would mind her taking that second job so she could raise the money she needed to get the new furniture. I knew it would be a heavy load for her, but she was always the one the hospital would call in on a short-call situation.

I asked her about how she would work the nearly eighty-mile drive. She explained that since she wrote the schedule for her department, she could make her days together for the three weeks the other hospital needed help. On the nights that she would work in the old hospital, she would drive up to her parent's home and go to sleep there.

I wasn't big on her driving nearly two hours up there and two hours back, knowing full well that she would work on both ends of the trip. It took some talking, but we decided she would do it. Judy could work long periods with no outward signs of stress when she was on a roll. I was getting so I could see those signs, but most people would never have noticed.

Everything went fine for the first two trips up there. I observed her and saw nothing unusual. On the last day she worked at the local hospital, she called me to tell me that her mom was going to have carotid surgery the next day. She asked if she could stay in the hospital with her until her sister could be with her a few hours later. I wasn't thrilled about this because I had worked a few long shift strings and knew that you need to rest when you have the time.

On the day of her mom's surgery, Judy called me to let me know she had made it back to her parent's home and was going to bed. I told her to get as much rest as she could and to call me later that night, and of course, we signed off with 'I love you.' While Judy slept, I did some work in the yard and then went to work.

She called me on her cell phone when she got to the temporary job to let me know that her mom had come home and appeared to be doing well. I told her about an accident we had just cleared out of the ER, where I was working, and hung up with our usual words. "Nurse stuff."

About 7:45 am the next morning, I got a frantic call from Judy. I heard a soft moaning in the background and asked her what was happening. "I just got home and found Mom on the kitchen floor, and there's blood all over. It's on the wall, the ceiling, and the floor. I've called the ambulance, and I'm holding pressure on her throat."

I called our now-adult children to tell them I was going to their grandmother's because something had happened. I asked them to be near a phone so I could call them when I had exact information. They asked me what had happened, and I said I knew exactly what had happened.

Her Mom had gotten out of bed during the brief time between her husband going downtown to get a newspaper and Judy arriving at their home. Apparently, she had dropped a kitchen utensil on the floor, and when she had bent over to retrieve it, the stitches on her carotid artery tore open. A moment later, her throat was spurting blood all over the kitchen.

About five minutes after I had left and was getting on the road to see her, Judy called me again. "She's still alive, but Verwayne, she's lost a lot of blood. I'm afraid. Please hurry!" I could hear the panic in her voice, and I pushed my speed.

I made the regular ninety-minute trip in less than seventy minutes and went straight to the hospital. The ER nurse directed me to the ICU room, where they told me I would find Judy. I walked down the hall and into her mom's room as quickly as possible. Judy was standing there, holding her mother's hand, tears streaming down her face and drenched in her mom's blood.

As soon as Judy saw me, she collapsed in my arms and sobbed. "I shouldn't have stopped for coffee. I shouldn't have stopped!"

I shushed her and just held her tighter. Over and over, I told her that this was not her fault, but she kept trying to take the blame. Her dad walked in, and I was shocked. I had never seen him so pale and shaken.

A few minutes later, we saw a helicopter land on the medical evacuation pad on the south side of the hospital, and I knew it was for her mom. Several nurses came rushing into the room and had us leave to make room for the incoming chopper crew. About the time the chopper was lifting off, Judy's sister arrived. I filled her in with the information I had learned and told her she needed to find her dad.

As soon as her sister was gone, I took Judy out of our car, pulled out of the parking lot, and returned to her parent's house so she could shower and change clothes. We were no more than in the car and alone when Judy told me what she had seen. "They didn't stitch her up properly. You know how they use a big mattress stitch on the end of something like that?"

When I worked in the OR for a month, I saw a lot of surgeries, so I knew exactly what she meant. They used a long stitch back into the vessel in a couple of places and then fine stitching along the edges of the blood vessel. Those stitches served as anchors.

After I nodded, she leaned toward me and whispered, "There was no mattress stitch in her artery! All I could see was the edge stitching. You can't miss that heavy mattress stitch. It wasn't there."

In the end, Judy was proven correct. Somehow, someone had neglected to place the two anchor stitches, and when her mom bent over, the finer stitches tore loose, leaving her to bleed out.

Her mom lived another three days before finally succumbing to the blood loss. Judy made it through the funeral, but I could feel the storm of emotions running through her. She never was one to socialize much, but she wasn't talking to anyone during the ordeal, not even me. I asked our daughter and son to help me keep her talking, a job that proved to be extremely difficult.

After the funeral, her dad pulled me aside and asked if I had time to go to see someone in the hospital, and I agreed. I followed him into the hospital and then toward the administrative offices. He walked in and introduced himself. A secretary told him he was expected, so we walked into the office of the principal hospital administrator and sat down.

The man started with a lengthy and sincere apology. My father-in-law never nodded, blinked, or spoke. The administrator admitted that there had been an error in the surgery's course. He explained that the hospital took full blame for the death of his wife.

My father-in-law maintained his silence. Finally, the man reached into a desk and pulled out a large brown envelope with five white packets inside. He handed them to my Father-in-law. I watched his face as he opened them. He looked at them and then gave them to me to see.

Inside each one was a check made out to each of his children. The first check I looked at was made out to Judy for just short of one million dollars. I didn't react because I knew where this was going to go. I opened each one and saw that each of Judy's siblings had a check precisely like hers. The last one was made out to her dad for three million dollars. I handed them back.

Her dad stood, handed the checks back to the administrator, and told him, 'Thank you, but no thank you.' He then walked out without another word. Once back in the car, he asked me, "Do you know why I did that?" Oddly enough, I did. I nodded.

He continued. "I've lost a wife. If I took that money, I'd lose a son within a matter of weeks. It's not worth it to me. I trust you'll explain this to my daughter?"

I nodded. I understood it was difficult for him to speak just then, but I knew why he had done it.

Judy's youngest brother was also battling depression and had turned to alcohol to find peace. It wasn't working out well for him. He had recently been evicted from an apartment because he had gotten so drunk that he was throwing glass bottles in the toilet. Naturally, it backed up the entire sewer system for the apartment complex.

He would borrow, steal, and lie to get money for his booze, and everyone knew it. Three years later, he would die of the side effects of alcoholism. A year before he died, he asked me to write a story about his last brush with death due to alcohol-related issues.

We traveled back to where they were holding the luncheon, and as we were getting out, her dad stopped me. "You are the only one who would understand why I did this. No one else needs to know. Do you understand?" I did, and I promised I wouldn't say anything. Eventually, the word got out to the rest of the family, but it didn't come from me.

A Change of Scenery

Somewhere in late 2004, small hometown hospitals began to be bought up by their bigger brethren. At first, this practice was good for the citizens of those small medical centers, allowing more big-town specialists to make once-a-week or monthly visits to the boondocks. However, all too soon, the larger facilities stopped offering essential services to the locals, turning the small hospital into a glorified band-aid station.

Maybe they cared they were making their clients travel further and further away from home to get services once done in their backyard—or perhaps they didn't. One by one, once-thriving small hospitals became nursing home extensions for bigger ones. Small-town surgeons were made to go to the larger hospitals if they wanted to continue to practice. The local ERs became aid stations, and the OB departments closed down.

Judy had worked for the same hospital for twenty-seven years in the same OB unit when word came down that her unit would be closed in a month. She would be given a choice of working in the Cardiac Care Unit or the ER. She had been an OB nurse for thirty-four years, and neither of the departments she was offered fit her desires.

Our children had both moved out, and we were alone once again. It was strange, but it was nice to have our privacy back. We had never lost the emotional or physical closeness we had enjoyed in our youth, and now we reveled in our freedom again. It was wonderful.

Don't for a moment think that we didn't enjoy our children, but we had done our job. We had successfully raised them to become useful adults. Our daughter was in the medical field, working at the same hospital as Judy. Our son had joined the Air Force, and he was becoming a shining example of the 'All-American Boy.' With that mission accomplished, we returned to our closeness and passions. That was even more wonderful.

I was working on a sports column I did every week for some local newspapers when Judy called me one night. I answered with the standard, 'hello,' and her first words were, "Arabian Trolley Cars." This was just before the ever-handy 'caller ID' feature, but I knew that only my wife knew that phrase. "We need to talk."

Judy had a hard time keeping her emotions a secret from me, and it was apparent she was upset. I asked her if something had happened at work. "I can't do this. You should see the memo they just gave me. I can't do this. I won't do this. We need to talk." I told her we would go out for breakfast and talk when she got home. We repeated those three words with all our normal passion, saying them the first few times, and she hung up.

I was up and ready to go the next morning when she pulled into the driveway. She handed me her bags, which stayed in the car while I put them in the house. She was silent as we headed to one of the quieter restaurants on the outskirts of town. Remembering our vow not to talk to the returning spouse, I stayed quiet myself.

Judy parked the car, got out without saying a word to me, and walked through the side door. I was about six paces behind her, but I knew she only used that fast 'nurse's walk' speed when upset. By the time I caught up to her and sat down, she tossed me an envelope, and I pulled out the note inside.

I scanned through the new Director of Nursing communication that was explicitly addressed to her.

> *Dear Judy, I regret to inform you that, as of February 14th, the OB department of this hospital will be permanently closed. You will be assigned to work in the CCU department, reporting to Jill Johnson. You will need to wear a green scrub outfit, as the pink scrubs you wore in the OB department are no longer acceptable. Thank you for your cooperation in this matter.*
>
> *Sincerely.*

I looked up, and I could see the fury in her eyes. In the thirty years we had been married, and I had never seen that level of anger in her. "They told me I could choose, and I told them I wanted to work in the ER. I don't enjoy working in the ER but detest working in CCU. I won't do it." Looking at her face told me she was dead serious about that statement. "I have ten days to do something about this, but I can tell you right now, I will not work in the CCU, especially under that nitwit Jill. What can we do?"

In the middle of my reading, a waitress who knew our eating and drinking habits had brought us both coffee and toast with jelly. Thinking of how my dad had always teased me about my coffee-drinking habits, I added my packets of sugar and cream and stirred the concoction to buy some time.

"Well, I was reading one of those nursing magazines you brought home. I see that there is an enormous demand for traveling nurses in OB departments all over the country, especially in Florida."

Judy cut me off, telling me that getting a nursing license in another state took time, and she didn't have time to waste. "I'm a step ahead of ya, dear. I also saw an ad for a license expeditor. Their ad says they can get you a license in ten days or less. It's worth a shot if you are serious about leaving your current hospital."

The look of disgust she shot me at that moment told me I had vastly underestimated her seriousness about leaving. But after pausing for a moment, I continued to talk.

"Alright. When we get home, you gather up all of your license materials and school credentials and jump into bed. I'll start making calls on this while you sleep." She reached out and held my hand, and the look in her eyes softened.

"So. How was the rest of your night? Pretty quiet?" Oddly enough, she kicked me under the table.

After we settled up for our breakfast bill, I grabbed the keys from her, and I drove us home. Once in the house, I told her to shower to help her relax and then go to bed while I made some calls.

With the sound of the shower in the background, I made my first call to an expeditor's office. A nice young man answered, "License Expeditors, this is Doug. How may I help you today?" I liked this guy.

I explained our situation to him, giving him some of Judy's career highlights. About the time Judy walked out of the shower, wearing just a towel around her hair, leaving me shaking my head and smiling, he continued speaking. "She sounds great, sir, but before I can go on, I need to get permission from your wife to allow you to speak on behalf." I handed her the phone, and while she talked to him, I lightly slapped her backside, getting that sly little smile I wanted to see.

"Yes, sir. You have my permission to talk to my husband, and I permit him to tell you nearly anything you need to know about me." She gave me a sneering smile and handed me the phone back. "Be civil, you goofball!" She exaggerated her hip movements as she walked away to the bedroom.

As Doug asked more questions, I heard her lock the bedroom door. *'Now, who's being goofy?'* was the thought that sped through my already occupied brain.

I spent the next forty-five minutes talking to Doug as he filled out his forms. He was able to check Judy's credentials on the nursing website of the state. Then he gave me a fax number to send him a signed paper permitting them to run a background check on her. I gave him my fax number, and he gave me his.

As he was speaking, I was already filling out the form statement he told me he needed. I told him, "I'll wake Judy up and have this signed and back to you in less than five minutes."

"Great! If everything works out and we get your form back quickly, I am going to walk over to the Florida Nursing License office, which is just half a block away. I'll process this immediately. You will need to send us a check for $450." I asked if they took credit cards; he assured me they did, and we hung up.

It took me a couple of minutes to wake Judy up enough to get her to unlock the door, but she finally rolled out and let me in. I had her sign the paper, and within fifteen seconds, she was sleeping again. I faxed the document to Doug, and I had only finished faxing the information to him when I received his papers.

I sat down to read what he had sent us when my phone rang again. It was Doug again. "Well, that was quick! Everything's good to go. As soon as we get your payment, I'll walk this across the street and get her license myself." I gave him our credit card number, and he read it back.

Doug then continued his speech. "Now, I need to tell you that there is a five-dollar processing fee to take this card over the phone."

I chuckled and told him, "Of course, nothing would ever get completed without a processing fee somewhere along the line."

Before he hung up, Doug asked me again, "What is her specialty field?" I told him she had over thirty years in obstetrics. "I thought that was what you said. While I ran that other background check, I got a call from an agency asking if I knew of an OB nurse. I told her I was setting one up right now. Do you mind if I give her your home phone number?" I assured him that would be just fine with us.

I was contemplating waking Judy up to give her the news when the phone rang. "This is Jo-Anne with American Nursing. May I speak with Judy, please?" I told her that my wife was asleep, but if she could call me back in five minutes, I'd have her awake and ready to talk. "I can call her back tomorrow if you'd like?" I told her that if I wanted to get smacked around by an angry wife, I'd tell you, yes, call me tomorrow, but give me five minutes. Jo-Anne laughed and promised to call right back.

I went back into the bedroom and once again woke my sleeping beauty. "A lady from a nursing agency is going to call you in five minutes. Wake up, dear!" I don't think she believed me right at first, but then the phone rang again. I answered and heard her feet hit the floor when I said, "One moment, ma'am, Judy will be right with you!"

They spoke for a few minutes, and then Judy asked me for our fax line number. I gave it to her, then listened a bit closer. "No, I don't know where that town is, but my husband will know. Yes, send the information and the job offer, and I'll send it right back. Thank you!"

Remembering that she was still only wearing that towel, Judy jumped up and down and hugged me. "I've got a job in Florida! They want me to start in ten days!"

The next two hours were a blur. Doug called back and gave me a temporary license number to provide to the agency. He promised me that when he got the permanent version, he would also send it to them. Judy and I looked over the proposed contract as we waited and couldn't believe what we were reading. They would rent us a place to live and pay all the bills except the discretionary things we might want or need, such as the Internet, cable TV, and food. They would pay her $34 an hour on top of all that, too.

When Jo-Anne called back, Judy told her she accepted her offer and told her to send us further information by email. A verbal deal was struck, and Judy hung up the phone. I saw her pause for a moment. She asked me about the speed dial to the hospital, but then she just dialed the number without it.

When the Director of Nursing secretary answered, Judy asked to speak with the director. "She's busy. You'll have to call back in an hour." I think Judy's exact words were something like, "Oh, to hell with that. Tell her I'll be down to see her in forty-five minutes." As I said, I had never seen Judy this upset, but she was happy to see that anger this time.

"What are you going to do, dear? You need to use some diplomacy here." I was wasting my breath. She was up and dressed already. We drove in the car to the hospital where she had worked for the past twenty-seven years. She walked down the hall to the woman's office and didn't even wait to be acknowledged.

"I'll not be taking that job in CCU. I told you I didn't want to work there." The woman tried to calm her, but Judy was on a roll. "I need to know when my department will officially be closed down, not that it matters anymore. You didn't give any of the OB staff any advanced notice. You just told us we would be moved around to other units. You've got over 150 years of OB experience in six nurses here, and you want us to change our life's work? I don't think so."

I stepped in and got Judy to sit down. The Director told her that the last official day of the department would be in three days. The last week would be time to clean up the unit. I saw the smile get bigger on the face of my wife. "So, my last official nursing duties here would be Saturday night?" The Director nodded.

"Let me make sure I have this straight, then. I already had Friday and Saturday off, so tomorrow is my last day in OB, correct?" The director nodded. "I have over 140 hours of combined sick days and vacation time accrued. I want that on my last paycheck. I want it on Friday. You were going to screw me, but I've already got a new job lined up, and I intend to be there." I saw the lady's eyes get bigger as Judy continued her rant.

"I've given my life to this place for nearly thirty years, and you were just going to dump me somewhere that I specifically told you I didn't want to go to. I don't care what you have to do. I want my sick time and vacation time paid. I don't care about what the taxes will do to my check; I want to be away from here for good. Goodbye." Judy stood up and was on the way out the door.

I stood and couldn't help but chuckle as I turned back to the hospital employees who had heard Judy ranting. "Now you see why I always just said 'yes, dear' all these years. Smart money would be to pay her. I think she's upset." I walked out of her office, apologized to the secretary for the scene, and asked if she could make sure that Judy would get her check as she had asked.

The girl hadn't been there very long but told me she would get it done, although it might have to come in two checks. I laughed and said, "I don't think she cares, do you?" and walked out. All I could think about on my way out the door was, *God, I love that woman.*

And Travel We Did!

I had a friend take care of our home while we were gone for the first year and on the road. I initially thought that we would be nomads for a year, maybe three tops. When it was over, Judy worked as a 'traveler' for eight years. We were into adventures, and her new job most certainly provided those. We met a lot of people, some very nice, and some not so nice, but we had fun. Somewhere at the start of the fourth year, we sold our house with the idea of moving to Florida for good.

Judy's new job counselor had told us never to bring more than we could safely carry in one car. We had a big 1999 Buick Park Avenue with a vast storage area. It took two days to decide what to take with us and another day to say goodbye to everyone. We were exhausted when we were officially on the road to Florida, leaving a circle of a dozen friends in the driveway.

Our original intent was to drive straight through, but we had time to kill before we could move into our new apartment. We pulled into a motel somewhere in north Tennessee and found an affordable room. As I remember, it was about ten p.m. when we checked in and about six a.m. when we left, but we both felt much better.

Our timing was just right, and we missed the lunch traffic jam in Atlanta. From there, it was a nice mellow cruise down I-75 to US-10. Her job was located along the Atlantic coast, north of West Palm Beach, so we took US-10 east to the I-95 bypass around Jacksonville and set the course south. If you've never driven along that stretch of road toward Daytona as evening began, you've missed some breathtaking scenes.

During a fuel stop, we could see the ocean, and at the first sign of a state park, we pulled off to soak our feet in the cold spring Atlantic waters. I remember the giggling, walking along the beach, and holding hands. We sat on a bench there and stared out at the vast expanse of water to the east, wondering who might be looking back at us on the other side, thousands of miles away.

Eventually, we made our way back to the Buick and looked at the Garmin I was using to guide us to our new home. When I checked it, it showed we were a little under four hours away. Remembering a couple of decades back when we had slept on the beach of Big Sur, we napped a little while in the car before heading south again. This time in a designated parking lot. Our wind-up alarm was in my bag behind the seat, and I set it to go off for two hours, and we fell asleep holding hands.

When the alarm went off, it startled both of us, leaving us sitting bolt-upright for a moment. We used the restroom facilities and walked along the beach one more time, finally getting into the car and heading south on I-95. The traffic was light, and the sky was bright with stars. As Judy peered into the night sky, she quietly asked me, "Do you think we are star-crossed? This all happened so suddenly; do you think this was meant to be, or will it lead us to a disaster?"

I thought for a moment and then laughed. "That 'star-crossed lovers' stuff is Shakespeare's gig. I've told you since we met we were destined to be together. Just keep smiling and looking for the good in life, and we'll probably find it." I felt her hand squeeze mine a bit tighter, and then she leaned back into the seat, her window slightly open. Moments later, she was gently snoring. She needed to rest, and it made me smile to see her face in the dim light of the night as we drew nearer to the next chapter in our lives.

Somewhere, about nine in the morning, the navigation unit sounded off about taking the off-ramp we were about to hit. I moved into the proper lane and waited for Miss Garmin, as I called my little blabber box, to give me directions. As it turned out, I saw the sign for the apartment complex before Miss Garmin told me about it. We soon found our turn and pulled right into the driveway, where I saw the office door.

We went in, probably looking a little worse for wear than most of the folks who already lived there, and found the woman in charge. In a scenario that we would replay many times, we produced our identification and signed a lot of paperwork, saying we understood the rules. Once we were 'official,' we got a brief tour and were finally given keys to our new place.

We had never been to a major apartment complex, so we drove around for several minutes to find our unit. When we finally found it, I looked back and saw where we had initially been parked. I realized I had left the circle complex in the wrong direction. Judy and I each grabbed a bag from the back seat, and we headed up the stairs and found our door. We did not know what we would see, so we took a deep breath, and I opened the door.

For several moments, neither of us said a word, and then Judy whispered, "Wow!"

The place was nicer than anything I had ever seen before. We had an enormous picture window on the inside of the backyard overlooking a large pond. There were two enormous bedrooms, a monster-sized kitchen, and a living room bigger than anything I had ever had in my life. As we walked through the place, Judy kept whispering to her, 'Wow!' while I was speechless.

It took us about twenty minutes to clean out the car and everything inside and into the middle of the living room. We both decided that was good enough for the moment. I had set the thermostat to 74, which was about ten degrees cooler than it was outside. By the time we had brought all of our stuff up, the central air had brought everything to a very comfortable setting.

We looked around and tried to decide what we should do next. We had spent the last thirty-four hours in a car, including our stop in Tennessee. Judy had to report for a three-hour orientation the next morning at seven in the morning. Finally, I asked her, "Remember the first time we were in Florida together? Let's take a shower and relax on the bed. What do you think?"

I waited too long for her answer because she beat me into the shower. By the time I got out, Judy was naked on the bed, lying on her belly. As I walked in, I paused for a moment to consider the beautiful woman that lay before me. She was now fifty-two, had birthed and raised two children, and was approaching the best part of her nursing career, and yet she still loved me.

When we were together, Judy was still the shy young lady I had met at McDonald's thirty-four years before. I always found her to be extremely beautiful, physically and emotionally. She had been a model mother to our children and a loving wife and friend. I could tell her everything, ask her anything, and she would tell me the truth. How could I ask for more? Some days, it made little sense that a woman like her could be mine all this time.

We ended up lying on the bed on our bellies, our hands clasped over our heads for several hours. After all of those years, we still found solace in holding hands. The touch of our skin always sent tingles of excitement through both of us. I whispered to her, "Judy, I love you. Do you realize how much I love you? Seriously? Do you? Can you even fathom how much I love you?"

I looked into her eyes and saw small pools of tears forming in them, and I suspect she saw them in mine. I could count on one hand the number of people who had witnessed me cry since I graduated from high school. Judy was the only one with whom I never felt embarrassed when she saw me do it. I call that love.

We reminisced about our life together. The successful happenings, the good, and the bad stuff. I was never one to talk about the bad things that had happened because I couldn't change those things. I found that talking about them very much always put me in a lousy mood and almost always left Judy outright depressed. On this day, we were able to talk about the house we lost and Judy's mom dying so needlessly. We talked about several other things that had happened without the gloom that came with those discussions.

As the sunset approached, I reminded Judy that we had a pool outside our first-floor stair landing. I remember both of us tossing things out of our bags before we found our swimming suits. She was going to pick everything up, but I told her I would clean it up in the morning.

We swam for a while, but our fatigue overtook us, so we went back to our apartment. I suspect we might have made love under normal conditions, but we settled for falling asleep in each other's arms. It was wonderful.

We spent nine beautiful months in that location before her agency put the action back into the term 'traveling nurse.' We got about three days' notice—two of which she worked—that Judy had been assigned to a hospital in Miami. I got our possessions out of the apartment and loaded them in the car. An hour later, we were off to the big city.

For a town that dealt with a lot of hurricanes and lightning, it amazed us we ended up on the twelfth floor of a twenty-story building. Interestingly, we were on the southeast corner of the Miami International Airport. It was a beautiful place with excellent facilities, but I soon realized that of the few thousand people living in the complex, I only found three other English-speaking couples.

Ever the gregarious sort, I made friends with some of the Cuban gents, and they took great delight in teaching me some Spanish words. Some of those words I soon learned weren't exactly the most helpful in the dictionary, but it gave them some laughs. They also worked with Judy on her Spanish but didn't teach her any 'bad' words. She gave them a list of words and phrases she used in the OB ward, and they gave her the Spanish equivalent.

After the gunshot belly wound, I could no longer eat fish because the oils in fish made me physically ill. I explained it to our Cuban friends, so they would often bring Judy various cuts of fish, and she loved it. One particular time, they brought her some lemon shark 'steak.' The Cubans cooked it up for her, and I thought she'd never stop talking about how good it tasted.

The area was overrun by once-domesticated iguanas. They were alleged to have escaped from a pet shop after a monster storm. When we went walking down by the river that came in from the ocean, you could see four—to five-foot-long lizards sitting in the trees. The things were pests of the biggest order, and people were always trying to kill them. I saw the mouth on one of them and decided I was never to be "The Iguana Hunter."

One February morning, my Cuban friends came knocking at the door quite early. It took me a minute to realize they wanted me to go with them. Never knowing what kind of prank they might try to play on me, I made a big show of being quite reluctant to go. After a few minutes, I relented and went out walking with them.

As we were walking down the street, one guy handed me a club that might have been a baseball bat in a former life. In its present life, it had a huge nail sticking out at the fat end of the club. I had no clue what we were doing, but I could tell by the chuckling my 'friends' did that it was going to be something real 'special.'

They took me down some of the back alleys of 'Little Havana' when one of them started shouting, and everyone took off running. I did my best to keep up, arriving about ten seconds after everyone else arrived. I saw them pointing just off the sidewalk in some taller grass, and when I looked, I saw a five-foot iguana lying in the grass.

Using body language, they explained I should take my club and kill it with the nail. I shook my head. 'No way!' Of course, this brought about another roar of laughter, and the youngest boy in the group, a lad of maybe twelve, brought his club up and killed the creature. Someone grabbed the thing as its squirming subsided and put it in a cloth sack, much to the approval of everyone in the group.

It was cold and damp that morning, and I desperately wished I had brought a heavier coat. We had been out for about an hour when we finally headed back to the apartment building. I was still clueless about why we had gone out to whack iguanas, but I admit I had had fun. They dropped me off near my apartment, and one of them told me in broken English that they would come back that afternoon. I thanked them, and they walked away, giggling hysterically.

True to their word, about 12:20 that afternoon, there was a knock on the door. When I opened it, five of the same men walked in and brought out a huge covered plate. They asked me if Judy was awake yet, and I was about to tell them no when she came out to the kitchen area, rubbing her eyes. They made a big scene of greeting her and asked her to sit down.

Judy looked at me, and I told her, "I haven't got a clue what they've got."

Once Judy and I were seated, they gave us a plate and a fork and placed chunks of meat on each of our dishes. Judy hadn't been with us, and I hadn't had time to tell her how I had spent my morning, so she took a bite. Her first response was, 'Mmm, not too bad,' and she took another bite.

The Cubans encouraged her to add some sauce they had brought, but we both knew we couldn't eat the sauce and still stand up later in the day. I never knew what was in their sauce, but it had always assured us plenty of time in the bathroom.

I had better things to do.

As Judy was eating her meat, they pressured me to try some, and after enough goading in Spanish, I took a bite — a tiny taste. In fairness to my friends, it wasn't all that bad, but by then, I knew what we were eating, and I was never much on eating a lizard. Our apartment was filled with laughter and howls for several minutes as they watched me pick up a piece and swallow it carefully. There wasn't a lot of chewing going on in my mouth.

Finally, they all had to go, probably to harass another friend, and they were gone, with the broken English equivalent of 'You tell her. You tell her.' Judy looked at me funny and asked what I was supposed to tell her.

I shook my head and stood up. "Well, don't get mad at me, but that meat was from some iguanas we killed this morning." As I suspected, she got mad at me, but at least I got some laughs out of the deal.

We had been in Miami for six months when we got the call that she had been assigned to a hospital on the east side of Tampa. This time, we had four days' notice, and Judy had the last three off work to help me pack the car again. As we were almost done, my Cuban friends came up, said goodbye, and hugged us.

We were saddened to part since, despite not speaking the same language, we had always had a good time with them. They had always been generous with us and had made sure that no one in the complex ever bothered us.

They helped carry the last of our belongings to the car. As we were about to leave, one of them pulled out their cell phone, and they took turns taking photos of our group. One of the younger men had opened the car door for Judy, and another opened my door. I started the car and rolled down my window to say goodbye one last time when the leader of the group stuck his hand in and said, "You are good amigos. Good amigos. We will miss our amigos."

I nodded and told him that Judy and I considered them to be our good amigos and that we would miss them. As we followed the parking ramp out of the building and headed to the northwest side of the airport toward I-75, Judy told me, "I'm not sure who will miss who the most. I think they liked us." I couldn't speak for them, but I knew we would miss them.

We lived on the northwest side of Tampa for three months and then moved to the northeast side. Judy had switched hospitals and didn't think we needed to move, but her agency did, so we moved. Six months later, we moved to Brandon, Florida, for her to fulfill another two ninety-day hitches. The place we had in that town was one of the most beautiful places we ever lived.

When we pulled in, I was sure we had the wrong address, but Miss Garmin had taken us to the right spot. Judy and I were never what you might call 'gardeners,' but this place had the most extensive variety of flowers I had ever seen. There was also a small creek that was filled with frogs and small fish that were fun to watch and listen to as they sang their tunes.

When the call to move to Ocala came three months later, I was dismayed, but we were gone in a matter of days. No disrespect to Ocala readers, but I never got to like the town. Our neighborhood was extremely loud, with parties, gunshots, and tires squealing.

I didn't go out much during that particular hitch due to an ankle injury I sustained while carrying our belongings up three flights of steps. Oddly enough, it healed just in time for us to move to Avon Park, a small town about ninety minutes south of Ocala.

We made our way down to the area and finally found the complex we would call home for six months. At first, Judy wasn't too sure that she wanted to live in the quarters. They looked like tiny dollhouses built in the late 1940s and early 1950s, but it wasn't long before we decided the place was all right.

The people who ran it were from Colombia, South America, and I remembered enough Spanish to talk with them. The place was kept immaculately clean, and the grass was always trimmed down nicely, which soon became a problem. It was hot there that late spring, almost insufferably so. The complex owners wanted the grass mowed twice a week. The only way they could find to do that without getting a severe case of heatstroke was to mow at six in the morning.

I had never been what you would call an 'early morning' person, and Judy needed to sleep after working a twelve-hour night shift. Eventually, we worked out a tradeoff.

The lawn keeper had come to our door, asking me to come to the office. In addition to the people who lived there by the month, they also had people who came in by the week. As I approached the office, I could hear a man absolutely screaming at them.

I took a deep breath before walking in and stepped into the waiting room. The co-manager asked me to explain what was happening, so I turned to the angry man. After rattling off a string of profanities, he told me he needed some 'new blankety blank-blank sheets.' I looked at the man and asked him to calm down, and I'd take care of it. I explained to the manager and his wife that he was asking for clean sheets. They weren't used to the extra expletives and thus didn't understand.

After they got him some new sheets, he started to leave, but I stopped him. "Are you going to thank them?" He gave me a look that told me that thanking them wasn't high on his list. I explained these people had been very kind to my wife and me. They would do almost anything for him if he could ask them without profanities if they had been given a moment. He looked at me for a moment, then stood aside, muttered a gruff 'Thank you', and walked out.

Our housing complex managers were happy that I had been able to defuse a situation that was about to get out of hand. As I was leaving, they asked if they could help me in some way. I told them about our sleeping arrangements and asked if there was a way they could mow on Judy's off days after eight in the morning. "No problem! No problem!"

That was the last time I heard a power mower outside my window at six in the morning.

Let's Move

The beautiful thing about this old-style complex was that it had the best swimming pool we ever encountered on our many travels. The bad thing was that the air conditioning units were almost as old as the buildings. If we tried to cool the unit down to less than 84 degrees, it would blow a fuse, but that's where the pool came in handy.

We joked about it a lot, but Judy liked to 'fool around' more than a woman in her mid-fifties than she did when we were in our twenties. I didn't understand it, but I was not one to complain. She would come home in the morning, and we would make love nearly every day. We would jump into the shower and then wander down to the pool for thirty minutes or so.

Early in the morning, we could sit in a pair of lounge chairs in the shade of the nearby palm trees, hold hands, and talk. It was a habit we had started long ago and practiced throughout the entirety of our lives. Once others showed up at the pool, we would go back to our little bungalow. Judy would go to bed, her big box fan running to provide some cooling and turn the radio on for background noise.

I was starting my serious writing career, so I would fire up the computer and work on various short stories. A few of them were printed in small niche magazines (most of which are now out of business, hopefully not from running my stories). I was still writing a sports column for several newspapers in Michigan and Ohio, so I kept myself busy indoors when it was in the upper nineties outdoors.

Judy had told me that the small hospital for which she was currently working had promised to renew her next 90-day contract, so moving was the last thing on my mind—until my cell phone rang. It was Judy's handler, and she explained that the local hospital had been forced to let all of its traveling nurses go due to a budget issue. She continued that the only place where she thought she had a job opening for Judy was in San Jose, California.

I think I must have said something not entirely under my breath because she asked me, "Excuse me? I didn't understand what you said there." I asked her when we had to move, and she gave me a possible start date a mere seven days away.

I asked when Judy was done working locally and was told that tonight would be her last night. I didn't say it, but I know I was thinking, 'Thanks for the heads up on that!'

The recruiter promised me she would call again as soon as she had something positive, but she told me we needed to get ready to go immediately. I woke Judy up, explained it to her, and asked her to call the hospital for more information. Just as she was about to call, they called her. Someone thought they would do her a favor and not have her work that last shift. Her job was finished there.

We were discussing our options and what we would do if the California job collapsed. Under the contract we had, we would have to leave our current residence in a week. I had just mentioned to Judy that there were three hospitals in town, and surely she could get hired in one of them when the cell phone rang. I let Judy talk to the recruiter to sign the deal, and then she handed it back to me. "She wants to talk to you about something."

This particular recruiter had been with Judy for about three years so far, and she and I had developed a good working relationship. "I know you haven't had time to talk with Judy yet, but you need to understand something. The job in San Jose isn't guaranteed yet, but if you are going to take it, you need to get going. I calculated it, and you will have to make 3200 miles in five days. Judy doesn't have a California license, so you'll have to go to Sacramento to get one."

I think she heard me sigh, and she stopped. "Is this too risky for you?" Everything in me wanted to say that it was too risky, but I told her that if she thought Judy would get the job, we would go entirely on her word. She told me she had a firm belief that the position would be Judy's if we got there on time. The job started on Monday, and if we started by the morning, we would make Sacramento by noon on Friday to get her license.

Everything hinged on getting the license.

I asked her to call me back in ten minutes so Judy and I could talk it over, and she promised she would. I explained what I had just been told to Judy, and she looked at me for a minute and said, "Let's do it." While we waited for the phone to ring, Judy packed our belongings. After moving so many times, we started living out of boxes and suitcases.

By the time I got the call from her agent, she had nearly everything packed. We sat and talked for a minute. We decided we would take one last dip in the pool and be gone. The walk down was a sad one. After initially not liking the place, we had grown quite comfortable there.

After a brief swim, while Judy dried off and changed, I told the complex manager we had to leave. They were upset and said they would always welcome us if we ever wanted to come back. I thanked them and went back to get dressed in my traveling clothes. I did one last check on the engine oil and radiator fluids, and we were off to see California again.

So Many Miles And So Little Time

As it turned out, leaving earlier than we had initially planned saved Judy's job. Making the run north to US-10 was easy, and we were soon westbound on US-10. We had been running in smooth traffic until we hit a massive stoppage due to an accident just east of New Orleans, causing us to sit for three hours. Fortunately, Judy was able to switch seats with me, and she got to sleep undisturbed by lane changes and other car movements.

Once we started again, we were soon into Texas, and for those who have driven across that state, it can seem like forever. Instead of state borders, we started marking time by reaching the next major city. We caught Houston in early morning traffic, then San Antonio in its lunch hour rush, before setting sail toward El Paso.

We arrived in the late evening, both drenched in sweat. Judy asked if we could stop at an inexpensive motel we found just outside of the west city limit of El Paso and got little argument from me. I smelled so bad that I was offending myself with my odor. We checked in, and while she was showering, I did a maintenance check on our Buick. All was good. Beyond adding some extra fluid to the radiator reservoir, the engine needed nothing. The tires had been new less than seven thousand miles before and showed no sign of wear.

By the time I went inside, Judy had cranked the air conditioning up and had finished her shower. As I prepared to take my turn in the shower, I reminded her we would pay for having it so cold in the room tomorrow. After living in the Florida heat for a few years, you learned that being too cold inside led to being unable to tolerate the temperature outside.

She laughed and told me, "I don't care. For just one night, I want to be cold again."

I had set our alarm for six in the morning. Once up, we took another shower and were on the road again. In almost no time, we were in Las Cruces and then Lordsburg. With the sun cranking up the heat, we drove into Arizona. By the time we hit Tucson, it was already 102 degrees outside, and the car's engine temperature crept higher on the gauge.

Rolling into Phoenix, the red indicator was to the far right side of its meter, but the sun was setting. I didn't want to chance blowing the engine up so far from anyone we knew, so once again; we found a small motel on the west side of town. I was concerned with the mechanical situation of the car but found that the fluid levels remained perfect.

I walked into the room just as the weather lady said that it had 'cooled off' to a mere 106 degrees. No wonder my poor Buick was upset.

The next morning, we rolled out of Phoenix just as the sun was coming up. It was still hot as a blister, but the closer we got to the California border, the more the temps moderated a bit. I had expected much heavier traffic, but we stayed at speed all the way to Pasadena. Things got sticky, but once we got headed north on I-5, it became clear sailing again as we drove along the west side of the mountains.

As we neared Sacramento, I could see that it was going to be nip and tuck to be at the licensing bureau before they closed for the weekend. I don't know how, but we pulled into their parking lot at 4:45 pm, so Judy jumped out with her paperwork in hand. When we got in there, two other girls were ahead of her. A waiting area sign said the office closed at 5 pm sharp.

Judy and I would talk about that afternoon for several years afterward. The girl at the window had forgotten one piece of her paperwork and was told to come back on Monday. It was 4:53 pm. The next girl stepped up, and the first thing the woman behind the counter asked for, the girl didn't have with her. She told the counter person she would be 'right back!'

It was 4:56 pm when Judy stepped to the window and handed her paperwork to the woman. She thumbed through the paperwork, saw the postal money order for the proper amount, nodded her head, and then did some work on her computer. In the background, a printer clattered, and a moment later, she handed Judy a temporary copy of a California nursing license. We thanked her, and she unceremoniously shut her window.

We were talking about how close we had come to missing out when my cell phone rang. It was Judy's handler, and the first thing out of her mouth was, "Did Judy get her license?" I told her we had a temp license in hand and explained how we had just beat the office closing.

She surprised me with her next remark. "Whew! Do you know how lucky you are? Apparently, the legislature has ended the temporary license law, and today was the last day you could get one without waiting six weeks."

I must have made a 'wow!' murmur because Judy asked me what was happening. The agency manager was still talking to me, and I couldn't explain just then. She gave me directions to our overnight accommodations, and I was scribbling as fast as possible on a scrap of paper. As our conversation ended, she congratulated us on making the cross-country trip and getting the license.

"What was that all about?" Judy was curious about the phone call. I told her I had gotten an address to a hotel about ten blocks from where we were just then. We were both tired, but the glow of getting the license made us both feel better. I wheeled the Buick out of the lot and headed down the street. Judy was in the process of entering the street address into Miss Garmin when the hotel appeared on the horizon.

I pointed it out as it loomed larger in the windshield. We were both exhausted from the long trip, and the heat and the thought of being able to sleep in for the next two days were welcome ones. It took about five minutes to get checked in, most of which was because the desk man had asked for my identification. No other hotel had done that, and it took me a minute to dig it out.

We carried everything into the room and sat on the bed; both of us were finally satisfied and relaxed. It was early in the evening, and Judy wanted to know what I wanted to do. "Why don't you take a shower, and I'll look around for where we can get something decent to eat." After all of those miles, I got no argument.

I heard the shower running and surprised her, slipping into the hot water with her. After several minutes of hugging and kissing, Judy got out. I heard her hairdryer running in the background as I washed my hair. About the time that her hairdryer went off, I stepped out and dried off. I told her to sit down on the bed and that I would be right out.

I walked out to the bedroom area with just my towel and found her wrapped up in her towel. "Do you know you made California history today?"

She gave me an odd look and asked me what I was talking about on the phone. I told her that the call from your manager, Karen, was telling me that, as of 5 pm today, California was no longer giving out licenses on demand. Judy had been the last person to get one.

We both started laughing and hugging. I then said, "See, I told you we aren't 'star-crossed.' We are on a mission." Suffice it to say that our hugging and kissing led to other things, and we spent the rest of that night in each other's arms.

It was nice to be close again and just to be together. We turned the air conditioner up and lay across the big queen-sized bed, naked, just as we had done some thirty-two years before. There was no moonlight, but an air of comfort made Judy relax again. Once again, it was beautiful.

We were to stay in San Jose for six months, and everything went well until our final ten days there. I had sensed that something inside Judy had changed. I couldn't put my finger on it just then, but she was different. Her agent had already talked to us about moving back to our last place in Florida, and we were eager to return to our old haunts.

It was a Friday evening, and Judy was on her way to work. Her routine had been to call me as she pulled into the parking lot just to let me know she had arrived safely. When her call came to me, something in her voice was off. I asked her if she was sick or just not feeling right, but she assured me that there was nothing wrong.

I could hear her footsteps as she walked across the hospital parking lot, but her voice was becoming softer with each passing minute. A moment later, she sounded more like an echo than herself. I kept calling out her name without much logical response. In the background, her footsteps became less of a pattern and more of a shuffle, and then I heard the phone hit the pavement and a heavy thud.

I could hear her breathing, so her phone must have fallen close to her face. I kept calling her name, but all I heard was an occasional moan. Suddenly, I could hear a voice in the background that got closer to the phone. I kept calling out Judy's name, and finally, another woman picked up the phone and asked if I knew the woman lying on the ground there. I told her she was my wife, but I was unsure what had happened to her.

I could hear more voices joining the group, and then I heard a sound that I was reasonably sure was a hospital gurney. I lost the call as they wheeled her into the hospital. I was agonizing over what to do when my cell rang again.

I found myself talking to an ER RN who was asking me all kinds of questions. I explained my medical background and did my best to explain what I had heard just before she fell. The woman told me that someone had observed her fall, saying that it looked like she had just dropped straight down.

We only had one car with us, but I finally found a young lady at the apartment complex who said they would take me to the hospital if I paid fifty dollars. I had no idea what a taxi would cost, but I just wanted to find out what was going on with my wife, so I paid her.

Judy was in the emergency room for well over three hours, and at no point did anyone talk to me. I understood they were busy, but it left my stomach churning as nothing else in my entire career had done. When someone finally did hunt me down, it was her shift supervisor who spoke with me. The doctors couldn't find any reason for her to fall.

They said that Judy had been attempting to talk, but nothing she said made sense. With only ten days to go before we left, the last thing I was going to tell them was that she might have had an emotional breakdown. I knew it might cause them to discharge her from her job and leave us stranded in California. I didn't need another headache.

It was nearly midnight when they discharged her. Judy walked out to the car with me, and I helped her into the passenger side and buckled her seatbelt. She would try to tell me something all the way home, but it didn't come out the way she meant. I knew they had medicated her, and I said to myself that it must have been the injections, but I knew better.

It took Judy about four days to recover enough to talk with the hospital manager. He told us that since her injury had happened after she had gotten out of her car and on hospital property, they would close her out on a compensation discharge. He told me she would be welcomed back if she stayed in California. I didn't tell him this, but we both wanted to get away from there.

I called my nephew from Michigan and arranged for him and his wife to fly out to San Jose. I would have them drive our car and possessions back to Florida. The last thing I wanted to do was to take a chance on Judy having an issue while driving. Worse, have a problem while we were in the desert, far away from help. The agency had called ahead and gotten our old place back in central Florida, and I called friends who picked us up at the airport in Orlando.

We had come back with little more than the bare essentials, but enough to get by until our car brought us the rest of our stuff. Once alone and in the comfort of a familiar place, we had time to talk about what had happened. Judy told me that something in her mind had told her she was someone else, and she blanked out as she tried to process that information.

I had her checked out by our old family doctor, asking specifically that they check her for a UTI. It came back clear, and all her blood work returned to normal. Late at night, she was talking to me, and I picked up traces of word salading again. Nothing like the first time, but enough that I was alarmed.

I spoke with the agency, and because the California hospital was paying the agency workman's comp, Judy could stay home in Florida for another ten days before the Florida hospital doctor cleared her to return to work. Between our arrival back in Florida and when she returned to work, I took Judy to five different doctors and had them examine her.

They all did various tests and compared the tests that had already been done, and they concluded that there was nothing wrong with her. I begged and pleaded for someone to take a closer look, but they told me I was wrong.

In the end, it was them that couldn't have been more wrong.

As I struggled to understand the things I saw in Judy, I went to visit a man I had become friends with a couple of years before our trip to California. At that time, I did not know his background, but I knew we had just clicked together.

Well over a year later, I learned he had been an ER physician who had been critically injured in a car accident and had been forced to retire. He laughed as I explained I had been an ER nurse, pointing out that we had a natural relationship because of our respective backgrounds.

I went to see him because I was seeing more changes in Judy that were scaring me, but no one else could see what I was seeing. We talked for an hour, and I explained something I had been seeing in her for a long time, almost from the time we had first met. I explained I wasn't sure if there was a medical theory for what I was about to tell him but that I had an opinion about her.

"I've known Judy for almost forty years now. In those years, I've found that she has three personalities, and which one would be in control depending on where she was at the time. When she was at work, she was 'Work Judy - Super Nurse.' Nothing could throw her off her job. Ten minutes after she got home and decompressed from her shift, she was 'Home Judy - Loving Wife,' perfectly content to allow me to run the show. She would be the sweet girl I had met so long ago."

But the personality I saw more and more frequently was 'Little Girl Judy,' the scared little girl from her childhood. It was scaring me to see her slide into that persona. My doctor friend told me that, while perhaps not in those exact words, my theory was entirely credible. Judy would slide from personality to personality to fit her situation. After I left his home, I wasn't sure whether I felt better or worse for having him back on my beliefs.

Six months later, the contract with the current hospital expired. Her agency had nothing pending for the first time in eight years, so she was put on temporary leave. With no local hospitals needing help, we found one of the hospitals in Michigan that Judy had worked with well over fifteen years before needed help.

A deal was made, and she made the trip to Michigan, where she would stay with our daughter. However, I had a contract with a side business in Florida that would keep me tied up for two months, so she went on alone.

That was a mistake I came to regret for the rest of my life.

Judy and I had never been apart for more than a few days in over forty-one years. We had always been there to support one another, kiss, hold hands, and talk. For reasons that escape me now, I elected to stay in Florida. She would call me every day and we would speak on her cell phone, especially as she went to and from work.

While we couldn't touch each other, we could say our three little words every day. Still, I heard 'Little Girl Judy' creeping in more and more often. I called my daughter, and she assured me her mom was doing fine, so I relaxed for a day or two. Then I got a call from Judy while she was at work, and she was crying.

It took me a minute to get her under control, but she told me she had made a simple—but nearly serious—med error. Not everyone realizes that medication mistakes are a lot more common than you care to believe, but in the course of her career, Judy had made very few. She also told me she was having problems calculating simple medication calculations. For most of her career, other nurses would come to her to verify a medication dosage, but increasingly, she was asking someone to check her work.

She begged me to come up to Michigan and get her, and the tone of her voice scared me. I jumped on a plane and was up there in three days. I had a friend pick me up at the local airport and drop me off at my daughter's home. After greeting my grandsons, I returned to where Judy was sleeping and woke her up. I looked into her face, and I felt fear creep into me. I kissed her and told her to rest and that I would be back in a bit.

I immediately went out to talk with my daughter, asking her, "What in the hell is wrong with your mother? How long has she been like this?" Again, no one seemed to see what I was seeing. Against my better judgment, I allowed her to go to work that night.

The next morning, I called the nursing supervisor and asked if there was a way I could take Judy with me back to Florida. She told me they had also noticed a considerable change in her work habits, and what they were seeing was disturbing them.

Three days later, we were flying back to Florida. I could already see a sizable change in my wife. A touch of confidence was returning, making me feel much better. She called the OB unit where she had been working, and they had a place for her if she could hold off two more weeks.

We filled out the paperwork and used the next two weeks to help her recover. When she finally went back to work, I felt much better about her.

Again, I was wrong.

Slowly I Turn

On the surface, Judy's return to work seemed seamless, but just as most people didn't see the changes going on before, they weren't seeing what was happening behind the scenes. The woman who had always been the sweetest thing I had ever known was becoming foul-mouthed and nagging about something that wasn't important or didn't even exist.

She complained about the dog hair all over her bed, but the trouble was we hadn't had a dog in nine years. She would point at a sheet and attempt to show me all the dog hair. I saw nothing. She spent a lot of time brushing down her sheets to rid them of the dog hair she insisted on them.

I often worked on a project on my computer while Judy slept. One night, she stormed out of her room to accuse me of pulling all of her belongings out of their cases and boxes. I went in to investigate, only to find that everything was safely in place. Judy looked at me with an icy stare and asked how I got all of those things back where they belonged without her seeing me do it.

I tried to hug her, but she said, in a voice that sent shivers down my back, "Don't touch me."

As soon as she was back in bed and sleeping, I called our doctor's office and explained what was going on. I made an appointment for the next day, but I also typed up a six-page report for the doctor to better understand what was happening before she saw Judy in the office.

Our visit lasted an almost unprecedented forty minutes, with Dr. Rodrigo in the room the entire time. At first, there was nothing there to support my claim that something was wrong, but then I said something that I knew would trigger her. To the average listener, the words were nothing worthy of even remembering, but they set Judy into a violent outpouring of words and threats.

All I said was, "Judy, did you figure out who made the mess in your bedroom the other night?"

As her hate-filled words poured out, even the doctor recoiled. No one else said anything, but Judy ranted on for nearly four minutes and then stopped speaking. Her hands grabbed her shoulders, and she began rocking back and forth, seemingly oblivious to us in the room.

The doctor tried to ask her a question, but Judy didn't or couldn't respond. The doctor then told me to get Judy's attention. I stepped up to her, wrapped my arm around her, and pulled her into me. Almost like we had stepped back in time, Judy burrowed into my embrace, her face deep in my chest. I saw the doctor mouth the word, 'Wow!'

Dr. Rodrigo stepped out the door and motioned me to step into the door frame so she could talk to me. She was worried that Judy wouldn't be able to work that night. I explained Judy wasn't scheduled to work for the next two days. Dr. Rodrigo stepped out of the room, leaving me holding my wife and doing my best to comfort her.

Several minutes later, a nurse came in and gave Judy an injection, explaining that it would help her relax. We then went through the checkout phase, where they outlined everything they had done and gave Judy a new appointment. Dr. Rodrigo tapped me on the shoulder and slipped me a note during this process.

The lady at the window was keeping my wife talking, so I stepped back and read it. 'I've made an appointment for Judy with a psychotherapist, and I think you both should attend it. All my best, Natalie R.' The note also had a phone number, a date, and an address.

Dr. Rodrigo stood at the far end of the hall when I looked up. I nodded my head that I understood, and she gave me a quick thumbs-up and went in to see her next patient.

"Are you alright?" Judy startled me with her question while I was thinking. I had been covering my mouth and holding my chin, subconsciously rocking back and forth. I wouldn't admit it to anyone, but the pressure was getting to me.

Once Judy was home safe in bed, I called the hospital and asked for Sheila, Judy's unit manager. I was surprised that Sheila answered the line instead of her office assistant. I explained what was happening, careful not to tell her everything I knew. I knew Judy wouldn't be able to work much longer, but I hadn't yet set our backup survival plan into motion.

As soon as I was done talking, Sheila told me, "Actually, I was going to call you here in a few minutes. The girls who have been working with Judy are telling me that something has changed in her since the last time she worked here. She's not the same 'Damn the torpedoes, full steam ahead' nurse she was last time. She is coming to other nurses to have them double-check her work and her dosages. Judy has never done that before."

There was little I could say to Sheila other than that I was taking Judy to another doctor the next day. She thanked me for calling and giving her a heads-up. I thanked her for listening and noting the heads-up information she had given me. I knew I would have precious little time to change our lifestyle, so I needed to begin immediately. I made a series of calls, immediately canceling as many services as I thought we could do without having them in our lives anymore.

My first actual book was about to come out, but I had to cancel some things that I had wanted to do with it before it came out. I cut our cable services and several other things I hated losing. It was entirely clear that Judy would not be able to work in a job that required her to be in charge of the lives of others.

We went to the psychotherapist's appointment, and it didn't take long for him to trigger her. Both of us sat back as Judy ranted for over five minutes about something that had not happened to her. When our time with him was over, he asked us if he could order some tests for her.

He explained that some of the testing would involve her being at the hospital all day and several other tests that could be performed at a nearby hospital. Judy, now a bit more subdued, agreed to the testing.

Two nights later, Judy suffered the event at work that I wrote about at the beginning of this story. She was working in the operating room, about to receive a newly C-Sectioned baby, something she had done a thousand times before. Just as they were about to hand it to her, she stiffened and fell backward.

She was taken on a gurney to the ER, where they discovered changes in the white matter of her brain and several other problems. As I spoke with the ER physician, he uttered a thinly veiled criticism, alluding to the point that I shouldn't have allowed her to come into work.

I blew up.

I reached into my wallet and pulled out seven business cards of all the doctors I had taken Judy to see over the last month and a half. I explained that all those 'fine doctors' had told me they thought I had the problem. I told him he should call these offices and talk with them. I had done every single thing in my power to get her checked out, only to be told they had found nothing wrong with her.

While I felt vindicated, I quickly realized that we were now out on fragile ice financially. I had no idea how long the hospital was going to allow Judy to stay working. I knew she shouldn't have been working with patients for several weeks, but my words were unheeded.

I would later bear the blame for leaving Judy emotionally unsupported for just over sixty days, but at that moment, I couldn't be saddled with the guilt that I should have stopped her.

Everyone knew what was going on with her. For weeks, her fellow nursing friends told the supervisor, 'There's something wrong with Judy.' I had told doctor after doctor that there was something wrong with Judy, but the doctors consistently told me it was me who had a problem.

It was terrible to be so right in all the wrong ways.

Fortunately, Judy had accumulated over a month's worth of vacation and sick leave. She would eventually go to work to do the jobs that kept the unit in supplies. For now, there were things around our home that she was content to do.

Judy had always been a purposeful house cleaner. When our kids were young and saw mom start to clean things, they found other places to be. It gave Judy that small bit of self-worth she had desperately been trying to find.

In the meantime, Judy was given her specialized tests. She was scanned, blood tested, and underwent a psychological test. Ultimately, the medical professionals all saw that something had gone wrong. The once dependable and robust nurse, who for forty-four years had stood tall, now had fallen. 'Work Judy - Super Nurse' had died, and she knew it.

Three months after her collapse at the hospital, we were called to the neurologist she had been seeing. Judy was remarkably calm, but I was a bundle of nerves. I knew she was aching to be told what she suspected; she could no longer work. I knew it was the truth, but I wasn't ready to hear it.

We went in and sat on the semi-circle couch he had in the office. He shook Judy's hand, then mine, and sat down directly across from us. The doctor reviewed his complete test sets and a sizable pile of papers. He used big words, extended definitions, and told of other tests he thought should be run. He then laid it all out on the line.

"Judy, after all of this, I can not recommend you continue to go to work. I'm confident you've known this for a while, right?" Judy nodded and sat quietly. There was no hint of surprise or hurt on her face. All I saw was a face of relief from her fears. She told me later that every night she had gone to work, her greatest concern was that she would hurt someone.

He laid out the problems he suspected and told me to watch for specific other developments. I nodded and asked him, "Can you tell me exactly who will listen to me? I don't know whether we could have prevented this situation or merely prolonged the ultimate ending of this situation, but for months, no one listened to me until it was too late. Who will give a damn about my wife at this point?"

I was angry, and I was hurt.

I had left my wife unattended for two long months, and I couldn't blame others when I knew exactly what had happened. I had put my desire to advance my company ahead of her well-being, and it came back to bite us both big time. Yes, the others involved in this scenario were also to blame, but the avalanche started when I allowed her to leave me.

As we left, the neurologist wished us well and said he would mail us some materials to help handle future things. It was a quiet walk to the car until I got back out on the freeway to tell Judy what the hospital lady had told me.

For a moment, Judy said nothing. Then she asked me, "What day is this?" I gave her the date, and I could see her thinking. "That's weird. I got my first nursing license on this exact day, forty-three years ago. Ironic, isn't it?"

I nodded, but one phrase came to my mind: 'Star-crossed.'

The Beginning of the End

It took several days for both of us to realize what had happened. For a stint, Judy was much more like her former self. I don't know what I was, but 'nervous wreck' was probably the most apt description. She saw herself as free from the worry of hurting someone, and I saw us in terrible financial peril.

We had just bought a home on a lake in Florida. It was a quiet and beautiful place. Judy had always had a 'short-term disability' insurance policy and a 'long-term disability' policy. I began to take steps to initiate the short-term policy. The hospital helped get that started for us, and about three weeks after we applied, Judy got her first check from them. For reasons that will become obvious, I will not name the 'insurance' company.

Thankfully, I had cut our budget to the bone several months before because her insurance payments were about 65% of her regular check. As soon as I saw the first one, I knew I had to cut even more things out of our life. At the time, we had been making a lot of money, a low six-figure amount, but we had spent like a low six-figure family would spend. Most of our free cash was spent when we purchased our lakeside home.

I had also been helping some people with their monthly bills now and then, but it had become a relatively large amount every month. I was not to become popular when I told these people we could no longer help them. It still amazes me how people who had taken thousands of dollars from us and had never attempted to repay any of it could turn on us the way they did. Some of them were quite vicious, savaging me on Facebook and other places. I learned from that experience.

Then there were the people who had been using the resources of my little business venture, expecting me to put in sixty or more hours a week helping them. They, of course, also turned on me. When something catastrophic happens, like that which happened to us, it will open your eyes to who was a friend and who was there only for the free beer. I tried to explain that my wife needed my help more than they did, but it was like no one was listening to me.

In early August of that year, my daughter had a problem in her life. She asked me if Mom could come up to help watch her two sons for three weeks. After a couple of hours of conversations, we agreed she could do it, and within a few days, Judy was on a plane back to Michigan. I already had a car up there, and I told her I would fly up in roughly a month and drive back to Florida together. At least, that was the plan.

As I was taking Judy to the airport, her short-term disability company called and wanted a lot more information. Judy answered as many questions as possible, and I explained the rest. The guy on the other end thanked me and ended with, "I'll see what we can do to get this thing back on track." He had hung up before I could ask him what he meant by that statement.

To me, there was nothing to 'get back on track.' We had statements from one of the finest neurologists in Florida. At least five physician specialists had agreed with the neurologists, and then there were all the reports from the hospital. Everything was cut and dry from my viewpoint. Judy had suffered a career-ending illness, and the specialists had written certifications stating she would never work again. I soon forgot about it.

I kissed my wife goodbye at the airport, and she was gone. I promised to see her as soon as possible, no more than four weeks from that point. Within an hour, I had returned home to take a nap and await a call from Judy, letting me know she was safe at the airport in Michigan.

Everything went smoothly, and she called me to say she had been picked up. Our youngest grandson was talking up a storm in the background as she was talking to me. There was a happiness in her voice I hadn't heard for a long time.

I wasted the rest of the day working on the next novel I intended to have finished in the next three months. With the new silence in the house, I was able to work on and off all day. Within a few days, I had made giant leaps in writing it, and I figured I might have it done within a month.

For about another week, everything was going well. Judy seemed happy with her daily calls to me, and I was writing up a storm. Then came the day we should have gotten paid by the 'insurance' company.

My first clue that something had gone awry was when the bank called me to tell me they couldn't process my house payment. I hadn't checked my account online, but it was the day Judy's disability payments should have been posted. As I explained that, the bank lady told me I needed to come down to talk with her. I promised her I would be down in ten minutes. I never checked our online balance.

When I walked into the bank, the lady who had called me met me and pulled me into her office. She explained to me that instead of the $1400 deposit we were expecting, we had only gotten a deposit of $329. Figuring there had been an error, I used the bank phone to call the hospital benefits office. I spoke with the lady there and then handed the phone to the bank lady.

When their conversation was finished, the bank lady told me that the lady at the hospital said she saw no reason that the payment to Judy hadn't been properly deposited and would look into it. Naively, I believed that because this insurance company had a reputation like a rock–no pun intended. Before I left, the bank lady asked me if I would need a short-term loan to help us through the mess while we waited for this situation to be cleared up.

I left the bank about twenty minutes later with a $2500 loan to help me get to Michigan, pay toward my house payment, and eliminate a couple of small debts before any future payments. I wasn't happy, but I wasn't in the peril I thought I was just an hour ago.

One more time, I was wrong.

I had scheduled my flight to Michigan for a Thursday, typically a slow day as far as Florida-to-Michigan flights go. I arrived in Michigan around four in the afternoon, and by five, I was at our daughter's home. Judy appeared to be doing alright, and it was wonderful to be there with her again. I sat with my grandsons and had a great time. Judy and I went to bed early that night and talked for the longest time.

Almost precisely at nine AM, my cell phone rang. The bank lady told me that our expected deposit had still not been processed, and our account was about one hundred dollars in the red. She didn't sound nearly as accommodating as the last time we spoke. I explained I was in Michigan and promised that I would call the hospital and get things straightened out.

Right.

When I reached the lady in the benefits office, she told me she was just about to call me. Judy's 'insurance' company had declined to pay her for those two weeks for reasons she didn't understand. I then asked her if she didn't understand it, how was I supposed to understand it? I had intended to start the trip back to Florida the next day, but I wasn't about to leave without having something resolved.

She promised she would look into it, but I got the contact number to pursue it myself. I knew she had other duties and people to care for, and I only had Judy and myself. Reaching the guy I spoke with a few weeks back took about ninety minutes. As soon as I spoke with him, I could hear the arrogance in his voice. He quickly explained that Judy's claim had been denied, and there was little chance it could be approved.

When I asked him why her claim had been denied, he laughed at me and told me, "She's faking this, and you know it." While I was trying to understand what he meant and why he would say it, he hung up on me. For the next three months, this guy would hang up on me at least ten more times. Every time I could get him on the phone, he became arrogant and nasty with me, as if our plight was a game to him.

Over the next few months, I appealed to every person, agency, and organization I could find. I was caught there in Michigan while everything I owned was in Florida. I had never intended to be in Michigan for over three days and had packed accordingly.

I had nothing except the things I had been able to bring up in a carry-on bag at the airport. I had a sizable coin collection in a safe in my house, but that was 1300 miles away, and I had no means to get back.

I'll cut to the chase to save the reader from reliving the agonies of what happened over the next nine months. We lost our house and everything we had left there. There were mountains of family photos, our car, my coin collection, all of our clothes, Judy's antique doll collection, and her wedding dress.

I had also left at least five computers filled with literally millions of photos I had taken during my years of covering racing and high school sports. There were many other valuable items I can't recall right now.

I tried to explain all of this to Judy, and things went even worse than I ever thought they could. We had lost a lifetime of memories, collections, and personal items that were never to be recovered. She was devastated, and all the work I had done to help her went right down the toilet.

She began to cry almost non-stop, and I had to take her to a doctor we had seen ten years before. He gave her an injection of something to calm her and some prescriptions to help keep her calm. I didn't blame her for being so worked up because I was barely holding myself together.

We had been turned down for help at every turn. We didn't 'qualify' for assistance from Social Services because she had made $155,000 in her last full year of work. Never mind explaining that most of that cash was sitting in a house in Florida that I couldn't get back to retrieve or save. They said that we should have had some money set aside somewhere. We were denied help and services every place I took her.

I was getting desperate since the things I had access to get some cash were charging me 40 to 50% for 'early withdrawal.' Call it what you want; to me, that was plain theft. Judy needed medications and medical help I couldn't get for her. My 'friends' for whom I had done so much work without ever charging them a dime wouldn't take my calls, wouldn't answer my emails, and had blocked me on Facebook.

Judy was almost gone from reality, and I wasn't far behind her. At about this same time, a congenital heart defect that I had had since birth was flaring, and nothing short of major surgery would fix it. I couldn't even get in to see a doctor about it. I was losing physical strength and hope rapidly as I became weaker. I even planned my funeral, right down to ordering my own headstone 'in the event.'

The doctor who helped me when this problem happened would still see Judy without charge. I took her in about the middle of our eighth month with no money coming in. During that conversation, Judy blurted out that she was going to kill herself. Our doctor friend asked her what she had just said.

Without blinking an eye, Judy told him, "I might as well kill myself. I'm worthless to everyone, and we can't get any help, and I'm a strain on my husband. I might as well kill myself. I'm a nurse. I know how to do it."

Within an hour, Judy was in a hellhole, also known as a psychiatric hospital. She was heavily medicated, and I was devastated to the bottom of my soul.

It took me eight days to get her out of that place. It was dark and dank, and you couldn't tell the staff from the patients. The only thing that came out of that ordeal was they got Judy on Medicaid for two months, mainly to make sure that the 'hospital' got paid for her stay.

When I finally got her home, Judy was a mere shell of herself. I could see her body, but her soul was gone. I cried for days.

As we entered our ninth month of no income, I got a call from the hospital in Florida. The lady from the benefits office told me I would receive a deposit from the 'insurance' company to the tune of $19,000 for past benefits within the next week. I told her I wasn't sure I still had an account with that bank. She told me that the bank had acknowledged the pending payment, which was surprising to me.

I laughed as she was talking, and she asked me why I was laughing. "Well, let me explain. Today is the last day I could have saved my house down there. I mean, talk about being a day late and a dollar short." She told me she failed to see the humor in that statement. I told her I had been unable to see the humor in the ordeal we had gone through over the last nine months.

My next question was to ask when Judy's long-term disability plan would kick in. I knew her short-term plan was over, but the long-term plan should surely kick in soon. I heard her clear her throat, and I just knew that the continuing kick in the groin wasn't quite finished. "While you weren't getting paid, Judy's long-term plan was canceled. There won't be any more payments."

Judy had carried that plan with that 'insurance' company for over twenty years, never missing a payment. There was nothing to do except sigh. The money we were getting was going to be an enormous help. Unfortunately, the bank was to get over $1000 of that. They continued to charge us $35 for everything that had come with no money in the account. This included them charging me three times every month for each time they tried to process their house payments on a house we no longer owned.

I spent some of the money getting Judy some of the medications she needed. I used some of it to see the heart doctor about my growing heart problem. He advised me I needed surgery immediately. I told him that not only could I not pay for the operation, but I also couldn't finance a newspaper anymore. I then made the mistake of saying something about getting that payment settlement to someone in the social services office. Two days later, her caseworker promptly canceled what little insurance Judy had.

I tried to explain it to Judy, but the mind can only be shocked so many times before it shuts down. Within a few days, Judy was wandering around the house, talking in nonsensical words and phrases. I knew she was on a rapid downward spiral, but I was helpless to help her. I held her hand; I hugged her. I must have told her I loved her two hundred times a day. It wasn't helping.

It was late March in Michigan, and while the weather was warming, it was still quite cold outside. There was a nice patch of woods about three hundred feet behind my daughter's home, and walking through those had always made Judy feel better. I had taken her out there twice in the last week to help her 'wake up.'

We hadn't been able to have dogs all the time we had been on the road. Somewhere along the line while we were in Michigan, we had picked up three of them from homes that no longer wanted them. Many times, when I couldn't reach Judy, the dogs could get her to smile again. They loved her without question and were attentive to her every mood.

One morning, I went to take a shower, and just before I did, I checked on Judy. She was sitting in a chair in the middle of our little living area. Feeling safe that I could be gone for a few minutes, I jumped into the shower. I noticed that Judy and the dogs were gone as I got out. I wasn't worried about it, thinking she was out in the kitchen getting something to eat.

When I got dressed, I went to the kitchen, and she was nowhere to be found. My daughter's home was enormous, with multiple wings and rooms. It had served as a nursing home when it was first built but had been closed for some reason. I went searching throughout the house, and I couldn't find her.

About that time, I heard the new black dog we had just picked up barking furiously at the back door. I did not know why he was outside, but he made it clear that something was wrong. He came to me and barked at my face, then ran away from me toward the woods. I listened for a moment and could hear the other dogs crying out as well.

Once again, the big black dog Buster was in my face barking at me, and he headed to the woods. He ran ahead of me and then would come back to me, barking as if to hurry me along. When I made the tree line,

I could see footprints in the winter's last snow and finally realized what had happened.

Buster kept urging me to move faster. He led me at least another two hundred fifty feet into the woods before I saw Judy. She was barefooted, dressed only in a thin flannel nightgown, and was knee-deep in the muck and water.

Our big boxer dog, Brutus, stood up to his chest in the water, trying to stabilize Judy as she swayed in fear and physical exhaustion. Hannah, a fat little rat terrier, was on the edge of the water, crying out as shrill as she could to hurry me along.

Buster leaped into the water and came to rest beside Judy, barking for me to follow him. I waded out into the cold water, fighting not to fall with all the muck sucking at my feet. When I finally reached my wife, all it took was one look into her fear-filled eyes, and I knew she did not know who I was.

As gently as I could, I embraced Judy and began talking to her softly, telling her I would take her home again. She was sobbing nonstop, asking, "Who are you? Where are you taking me? Who are you?"

I just kept holding her up and guiding her out of the swamp. It took me at least fifteen minutes to get her back to the house, where I got her into the shower to clean her off and clean her up.

I could tell that she was ashamed to be naked in front of a man she insisted she didn't know. I finally got her dried off, a new nightgown on her, and stood her by the room heater. I kept holding her, whispering to her, telling her I loved her, and apologizing for allowing her to get out to the swamp. My tears streamed down my face, just as they are as I write this moment down for you.

Once again, I had let my wife down, and my carelessness had nearly been fatal. If it had not been for the love of the dogs and Buster's relentless urging for me to follow him, Judy would have tripped in the swampy water. As weak as she was, she surely would have drowned. There wasn't a doubt in my mind that she had been mere minutes from death.

It's incredible to me that 'dumb animals' care more for their humans than most humans care for their humans.

The Final Time

I hoped that after a day or two, Judy would snap out of the emotional coma that had engulfed her. But it didn't happen. She realized who I was, but she didn't respond to me as my wife had always responded to me. I would talk to, hold, hug, and tell her I loved her, but she had very little to say to me.

She was sinking into the worst bout of depression that I had ever seen her experience. Her voice was as flat as a tabletop, devoid of emotion. She didn't want any physical touch, even to the point of not wanting to be touched by our youngest grandson.

Our entire relationship had been filled with holding hands, hugging, and kissing, and now Judy wanted nothing to do with that behavior.

Three days after her swamp affair, I noticed Judy was talking to herself, and none of it made sense. We would go to bed at night, and I would find her wandering the house in the middle of the night. I was becoming more and more concerned, but it was the morning that Judy told me that the dryer was speaking to her.

She said it told her that our oldest grandson was smoking 'dope', and I knew I had to act. Marijuana has a very distinct and difficult-to-remove odor, and I didn't smell it in the house or on him.

After the grandsons were off to school, I gathered Judy, got her in the car, and headed to the hospital. I debated about just seeing the doctor or going to the ER. I had decided to go to the doctor's office and was about five minutes away when Judy suddenly sat forward. I asked her what was wrong, and she looked at me. "Did you hear that guy on the radio? He just told me to cut myself. Why would he say that to me?"

I changed my course to the ER.

As I go forward, I need to be careful here. This was a hospital where Judy had worked for a long time. The woman who was the head nurse that day was a woman with whom I had worked but had never liked her. In my opinion, she was not a professional acting nurse.

When I told them what was going on, it was that nurse who decided that she would handle Judy during her stay in the ER. For purposes of this story, I'll call her Nurse Smith.

We were taken to a room, and Nurse Smith began seeking information from Judy and me. She asked questions in a loud and flippant tone of voice designed to be heard throughout the ER area. I asked her to lower her voice at two different points. After she took Judy's vitals, she left the room. Moments later, a young doctor came in to talk to her.

He listened to my version of what was going on and then spoke with Judy. He was in the room for about three minutes. Once he was outside the room, Judy and I could hear Nurse Smith telling the doctor that Judy had always 'been crazy,' and it was nothing 'unusual' for her. Judy turned to me and asked, "Why is she saying that? Why is she telling him that?"

Judy began crying after hearing those words, and she was crying when the doctor came back in. He was telling me I should take her back home and fill a prescription to give her. He hadn't ordered any tests. In the 'business,' it was the standard 'treat and street' treatment. I told him he wasn't going to blow us out of the ER quite that easily.

In retrospect, I should have kept my mouth shut.

The doctor left the room, and we could hear Nurse Smith telling the doctor many things, most of which weren't true. The next thing I knew, he was back in the room with us. In his best, 'I'm the doctor, please listen to me' voice, he told me he wanted to send Judy back to the hellhole psych ward that she had been in just a few months before. I told him there was no way she was going back there. I wanted her treated, but not at that facility.

I explained the conditions and the shabby way Judy had been treated and that I would not allow her to be taken there again. As we were talking, I saw Nurse Smith lurking just outside the treatment room door, soaking up my words. I later learned she had zeroed in on two words, 'taken there.'

We had stayed in that room for almost an hour before Nurse Smith stepped in. I should have known I was being set up when I was asked to see someone in an upstairs office. I should have known it, but I wanted Judy to be treated with care. I was really hoping for her to be admitted and treated as an inpatient at that hospital.

I left the room, went upstairs, and waited for the person I was told wanted to talk to me. I finally asked someone where that person was and was told she wasn't working that day. I immediately headed downstairs and found that they were going to send Judy to a different facility.

One of the ER aides told me the ambulance was about to take off with her. I had no problem with that because my only concern was to get Judy the help she needed. I kissed Judy as she was being taken to the ambulance and told her I would be down as soon as possible.

Having a few years of experience in the ER, I asked the ER secretary if there was anything I needed to sign. She looked at the paperwork and told me my daughter had taken care of it. While I had no problem with our daughter signing any papers, I found it odd because they knew right where I was. They also knew the person they had sent me to see wasn't working. As I left, I was told Judy wouldn't be allowed visitors for the first twenty-four hours. That made sense to me, so I just went home.

The next day, I drove fifty miles to the hospital that was treating my wife. When I spoke to the woman at the desk, I had my identification ready to give her when she looked up at me. "You've been banned from seeing your wife, sir." I asked her to repeat that, and once again, she told me I had been banned from seeing my wife for ten days. I smelled a rat, and I suspected I knew the name of the rat.

I asked why I had been banned, and no one could give me the reason, but eventually, I was sent to a man in charge of the unit. After speaking with him, I found out that the paperwork my daughter had been duped into signing contained a clause that only she could visit Judy. It also said she didn't want me to be allowed to see Judy.

That was pure hogwash, and I told the man, "Sir, while I respect you, you underestimate me. I know the system and how it's played. You can let me in now, or you will wish you had." He said he understood but was legally bound to follow the signed statement.

It took me three days to gain access to see Judy, and when I did, I saw that the only thing remaining of her was "Little Girl Lost Judy." Her face was devoid of features, and she was almost robotic in her motions. I went into her room, a ward that housed four female patients and reached for her hand. As I touched her, Judy recoiled as if I had electrocuted her until she looked up and saw me.

When she realized who I was, she broke into a sobbing fit that tore my heart out. I held her close, and she kept whispering, "I knew you would come. I knew you would come. I knew you would come. Thank you for saving me!"

I spent about two hours with her and saw her becoming herself again. I was telling her that visiting time was almost over when a young girl came to her room desk. She slipped a paper to the bottom of a stack of documents already there.

I looked at the clock, and it was 4:05, five minutes after visitor hours were technically over. I picked the paper up and started reading, but I quickly had to sit down to keep from falling. The paper was a notification of a court hearing scheduled for 8:30 the next morning.

The paper said that some hospital doctor recommended that Judy remain for treatment for a 'period of at least sixty days, but no more than ninety days.' I was horrified. If I had not been there late that day, I would have never seen that paper saying some doctor that I later learned had never even seen Judy was going to lock her up for two to three months.

I went to the nursing desk and was told I needed to leave as visiting hours were over. I held the paper up and asked where and how this had happened, and again, they told me to go. I did my best to restrain myself, but I would be back the next day, and they would learn the meaning of the song, 'Ain't No Mountain High Enough.'

I was ignored.

The paper had the number of the 'attorney' allegedly representing my wife, and I started calling it as soon as I was out of the hospital. Over the next five hours, I called that number at least twenty times, leaving a message that I wanted to speak at the hearing on behalf of my wife. He never returned my call.

I was in the courtroom about an hour before it started. I wanted no part of any shenanigans where they might sneak her in before I got there. I wasn't allowed into the courtroom, but I could hear the proceedings going on inside, and the only words I could think of were 'Kangaroo Court.'

No one showed up on behalf of a single patient, and each was given the recommended sixty to ninety days of further 'treatment.' Each case lasted about two minutes at the most. My stomach was churning like a cement mixer.

About the time I thought perhaps they had already brought Judy down, she was brought to the waiting room where I was sitting. She was not exactly shackled as a criminal, but as close as they could get short of having a belly chain. She had cuffs on her legs and arms. I saw she had been crying, but she sobbed franticly when she saw me. "You came! You came! I was afraid that you weren't coming, and they told me upstairs that you weren't coming. I was so scared. I was so scared!"

I wanted to hug and hold her, but a woman in a uniform wouldn't let me. I whispered to Judy, "Baby, I'm here, and I promise you this will not happen. I love you, and you will go home with me. I promise."

The female guard looked at me like I had given her a social disease, but as I had told them a few days before, they had underestimated me.

A group of people were ushered in who were going to be 'sentenced' along with Judy. They weren't happy about it, but I was allowed to go in. I was forced to sit in the back row of the court. It took me about two minutes to figure out who Judy's attorney was. He was the quiet one sitting in the row just in front of me.

During a brief intermission due to some doctor who was late to arrive at the hearing, I leaned forward to tell the man who I was. I told him I wanted to speak for my wife. He shrugged his shoulders and turned around to face the front of the courtroom. As if I wasn't already worried enough, seeing how this coward had dealt with me and how he barely said four words on behalf of his other 'defendants' sent a bolt of fear through me.

As it turned out, Judy was the last case on the docket. Some doctor stood and was sworn in, and he stated it was his professional opinion that my wife needed to stay for at least sixty days, perhaps as long as ninety days. It was the same thing he had done with each case before her. When the judge asked her 'attorney' if he had anything to say, he mumbled, "No, sir," and sat down.

I immediately jumped to my feet and shouted out, "I have something to say." Everyone in the court stared at me as I stood there.

The man allegedly representing my wife finally found his feet and told the judge that 'Mr. Greenhoe has called me multiple times, asking to be able to address the court.'

As I stepped forward, I said loud enough for everyone in the court, "Yes, I called you about twenty times, but you never called me back. Thanks for that courtesy."

I looked over at Judy and saw genuine fear on her face, and suddenly, my fear left me. The judge asked me what I wanted to say. "Your Honor, my wife will not benefit by remaining in this facility. They don't allow her to be touched here. We have held hands and hugged all our lives. My wife will not thrive if she is not touched. I can take care of her, and she will get better."

As I looked around the room, it was plain that no one had ever spoken to this judge as I had done before. "Since I've been here, I was told that she had a severe urinary tract infection that was entirely missed by the referring hospital. I know very well from my medical training that a UTI will cause the symptoms that Judy exhibited at home."

The judge looked at the doctor who had testified about her problem, who did probably the first honest thing he had done all day. He nodded his head that I was correct.

I continued with the theory of 'in for a penny, in for a pound.'

"As long as you are communicating with that doctor, Your Honor, ask him if he has, at any point in time, ever seen my wife before she appeared in this court." A small giggle went through the courtroom because everyone there knew that the doctor doing the testifying had seen none of those patients. I knew he was going to bill them for his time later. It was part of 'the game.'

I started to talk again when the judge broke in. "Are you trying to tell me you can care for your wife better than the doctors in this facility?" I nodded, and yes, I could. "Are you telling me you want to take your wife home with you, regardless of the recommendation that the doctors of this facility say that she should stay here?"

Again, I told him in the loudest, clearest voice I could muster, "Yes, Your Honor. That is *exactly* what I am telling you. I can care for my wife much better than she is being treated here." A courtroom-wide gasp went up. I continued to stand straight and looked the judge in the face. I could see the anger boiling inside him.

The judge held his gavel, and I wasn't sure whether he was going to bang it on his desk or throw it at me. I doubt he knew which action he would take, either. Finally, he gathered himself up and spoke to me. "Mr. Greenhoe, I want you to get your wife, and I want you to get out of this courtroom. I want you to get out *now*. Get the hell out of my courtroom and take your wife with you. *Get out!* **Now!**"

He stood up and left the room.

I suddenly had court employees surrounding me, a couple shaking my hand, and more than one whispering to me they were afraid that the judge was going to send me to jail for disrespecting him. I told all of them that at no point in time had I disrespected the judge. It was his court that was disrespecting my wife. Another gasp went through the people still in the courtroom.

As I had told them, *'Ain't No Mountain High Enough.'*

I later got a video disc of that day somewhere, and the judge probably had considered putting me in jail. Still, I believe it was me maintaining control of my emotions—and the judge losing control of his—that kept such a thing from happening. It didn't matter to me because my wife was going home with me.

It took them almost an hour to get Judy 'checked out' of their facility. At one point, they deliberately separated her from me so they could attempt to get her to stay with them. Later, Judy told me that when they tried to convince her to stay, she told them, "No way. You can go to hell. I want to be with my husband."

When we walked out, the head nurse of the unit was there to say something to us as we left. I listened to her first six or seven words and cut her off. "You know, ma'am, no disrespect, but this place would be a great place to start a psych ward."

She stepped back as if I had slapped her. I took Judy by the hand, and as we walked out the door, I yelled, "We'll see you in the funny papers!" I suspect that didn't go over well, but I didn't care if they liked it or not.

All the way home, Judy held my hand. About twenty miles into the trip, I could see her face fill with life again. After another fifteen miles, I heard my dear wife laugh for the first time in a long time, and I knew she would be alright. The dogs, those precious animals that had saved her life, were thrilled to see their 'momma' again.

We got home about one in the afternoon. The first thing we did was to take off our clothes and lay skin-to-skin in each other's arms, with the dogs lying beside us. We must have whispered our three words to each other one hundred times. We were safe, and we were together and going to be alright.

And for a while, we were.

The Long and Winding Road

For several months, Judy was much more like the woman I had known all our time together. We held hands and kissed as we had always done and said our three words at every parting. It was a wondrous time for us, but then she began to change. We would talk, and she would forget the topic of our discussion.

I know you might think, 'Well, everyone does that!' Indeed, they do, but this was different. Judy would head out into the kitchen, and I would find her a few minutes later, still standing in a hallway. She would be unable to recall where and what she was going to do. I would ask her, "How are you doing, Judy?" For the briefest moments, I would see a flash of fear as she tried to remember who was talking to her.

It happened in small increments. Her memory and ability to recall things would downgrade a bit at a time. Just about that time, I thought, 'Alright, she's stabilized,' Judy would slip down again in an unfamiliar area. At one point, her ability to speak was impaired, but that was just something that seemed to correct itself a few days later.

I took her to see three different specialists, and all of them told me it was just part of the 'natural progression' of dementia. I asked if I could help her fight this somehow and was told to keep talking to her—to engage her—even when she didn't seem to understand me. The goal was to force the brain to maintain or rebuild motor neurons and hopefully slow her descent into an isolated and hopelessly confused mind.

I worked to talk with her two or three times a day, often reading my stories as I wrote them to her. I would ask for her opinion on some things we had talked about, and sometimes she answered my questions, and sometimes, I would get nothing but a blank stare.

I did my best always to smile and never become impatient with her. This woman had been my mate, lover, and best friend for most of my life. The very least I could do for her was show her all the 'tender mercies' I could. I had people ask me why I didn't put her 'in a home.' I told them I had the training and strength to care for her at home, and my wife would live with me. I know that not everyone can do that, and I am grateful for the time it bought me with her.

Judy gradually became more confused for longer periods, but I did my best to keep her comfortable and safe. There were times when she was

'Sweet Loving Wife Judy' for a time, but all too often, I saw 'Frightened Little Girl Judy.' She would love to take a walk in the woods or, once we moved to the Upper Peninsula of Michigan, around the beautiful lakes, streams, and waterfalls that are so abundant.

Over time, Judy's gait changed from that fast 'nurse's stride' to a slower, unsteady walk. I would always hold her hand and steady her as we strolled down our sidewalk. The exercise was good for her, and it gave us time together. After a lifetime of holding her hand and talking, I still wanted to be with her, walking and talking together.

In the course of her life, Judy was rarely ill. She was injured a few times, but her missing a scheduled shift due to illness was an absolute rarity. As her dementia and Alzheimer's advanced, I had to be sure that she didn't develop a pneumonia infection. She had always been one to sleep flat, but it became necessary to have her sleep in a recliner to keep her from coughing all night.

One of her doctors gave us a standing order for her to take an antibiotic that specifically targeted lung infections as they began to develop more often. One of the college classes I loved was Microbiology, the study of bacteria and viruses. That knowledge helped me know when an antibiotic would be useful and when you just had to wait it out. Taking an antimicrobial willy-nilly isn't good for the body, so I used all the 'due care' I had learned over the years.

There were times when Judy's blood work would show that she was extremely iron deficient. We would have her get ferrous infusions to help bring her back up to normal. I did everything I could do to keep her healthy, but there is an extent to the amount of help you can provide as life winds down. We fought the fight the best we could and never was a time when I didn't love her and care for her.

And The Rest is Silence

From the time I started this story, I kept asking myself how I would end it. Knowing the nearly inevitable path of patients with dementia, you can figure out where this story will end or has ended. I don't care to recall or relive any part of that projected ending. I'll leave that part for you to decide. Like female attire, what is left to the imagination is always better than reality.

I've always been a fan of Shakespeare, and of his works, 'Hamlet' has always been my favorite. This chapter's title uses Hamlet's last words as he is about to die. Without trying to bore you, allow me to give his last words in their totality.

O, I die, Horatio;
The potent poison quite overcrows my spirit
I cannot live to hear the news from England
But I do prophesy the election lights
On Fortinbras; He has my dying voice;
So tell him, with the occurrents, more or less,
Which have solicited - The rest is silence.

Hamlet is dying, stabbed with a poisoned sword. He tells his best friend Horatio to tell his story to Fortinbras, hoping to help him become the next king of Denmark. In this story, I have played the role of Horatio, Hamlet's best friend, or, in this case, my wife, Judy. I have told her story, although, in many places, it was painful for me to do so.

In her waning years, Judy struggled to remember her life. She always worried that she could never do enough or be enough. She seemed to believe that her life had never been used to do enough good. Every time Judy told me, 'I don't remember,' I would tell her, *"I remember, Judy,"* and tell her the memory she was trying to recall.

Her biggest fear was never having done enough for others. It was my job to remind the world of what she did and assure her and you she was, indeed, enough. Judy was a natural mother, a woman with strong nurturing skills. It was one of the many reasons I loved her so much.

Our home was always a place where all the neighborhood kids flocked. Many times, a young neighborhood girl would visit my wife to ask about the things that were happening to her. They trusted her to give them straight answers without the hype. She would urge them to talk with their mothers, but more women than you can imagine don't understand those things either.

At her job, several doctors I knew always told me that when the life of a mother and baby were on the line, it comforted them to look across that table and see Judy there. She was always unruffled and unfazed, a natural when it came to helping a woman get to the actual delivery situation. She knew how to maneuver women to get the baby moving. One doctor, in particular, would call her at home to ask her to come in and do that 'Judy thing' she did to get the woman delivered.

The thing that probably saved us from having more than two children was the fact that she got to hold babies almost every night she worked. She loved babies, and it was plain that babies loved her. Instead of allowing them to lie in a crib at night, if the baby were awake, she would hold it and talk to it. She would tell the little one it was a crazy world out there, and it had to grow up fast and be smart.

My wife was an exceptional mother to her children. Without and yet still totally bragging, both of our kids were top of their classes. One of our daughter's instructors told me she was among the best debate students he had ever seen. 'She even scares me!' he told me.

She became a nurse assistant and went up from there. She has had two children of her own. Judy always worried that she hadn't done enough to raise her, but I told her to observe how she was raising her son. A girl raises her family based on how she perceived she was raised.

My extremely biased opinion is that our grandsons will be just like their mom: strong and opinionated, unafraid to tell you where they stand. They don't 'feel' anything; they 'think' things. If you ask their opinion on a subject, they will start saying, "I THINK this...."

Our son was homeschooled from third grade to his freshman year. He wanted to return to public school to play high school football. When I tried to enroll him again, they tried to put him in seventh grade instead of as a freshman. I refused to allow that. I finally struck a deal with the principal that he be given a six-week trial with his age group. If he couldn't cut it, I would allow them to place him where they saw fit.

At the end of the six weeks, Skip was top of his class and stayed there all his high school career. He scored extremely high on his armed forces test and was invited to join the Air Force. He was also top of his class there and served with distinction in his deployments abroad.

He later became a paramedic in a major city and is now an RN, intending to work in an ER in that same town. From what I heard from some friends, he was a good one.

I would love to tell you I played a major role in their rise to the top, but I know it was all my wife. She held them to a better standard in life. She demanded our daughter behave a certain way. Yes, they had disagreements, but in the end, Mom always came out on top.

Both our son and our two grandsons know the answer to the question she would ask them: 'Good boys become?' The response better be quick: 'Good men!' It's not only girls who must have standards. Boys need to know they have a lot of responsibilities in life, and she saw it as her job to make sure that they knew that.

Finally, Judy was not only my wife; she was my best friend. I could tell her anything. When I was afraid, she was there to comfort me. Our love wasn't only strong; it was true. From the very start to the end, there wasn't a single moment when we didn't love one another. You could count on one hand the number of times we spoke crossly to each other.

Even in her decline as her condition became worse, I could never find it in my heart to answer her abruptly, even when the questions became repetitive and frequent. Without a doubt, I know that if the roles had been reversed, she would have done the same for me.

Those vows we made back on the bed of a Florida hotel, naked in the moonlight, kept us strong enough to get through all that life threw at us.

To end it right, Judy was not only 'The Story of My Life,' she was 'The Love of My Life. No one else even came close, and as I said in the beginning, 'I will love you forever.'

Time engraves our faces with all the tears we have not shed. - Natalie Clifford Barney

Epilogue

Toward the end of this story, I couched my words. There are many memories I want to relive by writing them here, but there are also memories best left to my wife and me. For the story's purposes, a detailed description of the slow loss of the beautiful soul that was my Judy is nothing more to be gained. I did my best to reveal what needed to be known. Anything more would be nothing more that the reader has not already realized.

As I was writing this story, I sent it to various people I use as 'beta-readers.' These people got my story as I wrote it, with my only requirement being that they give me feedback on what they were reading. One such reader asked me how accurate this story was, alluding that I might be 'prettying it' up for the story. In a way, he was right. I didn't include a few of the bad things that happened along the way. It added nothing more to the story.

Judy had several other incidents along the way, most very small, but there were three or four severe events. I eventually decided that there would be nothing gained by including them here. This story is about 95% true, with occasional romanticizing of some events. We had a relationship that was something special, but I don't say that to imply that relationships others may have had are not special. I just knew that our lives were worth being together.

Along the way, Judy saw several therapists who helped her. We also saw far too many people that should tend to their problems before charging others to listen to the other's problems. There was one such female therapist that we both walked out on when she flaunted her 'power over us.' I reported her to the head of the group that employed her, and several weeks later, I heard she was no longer working there. It could have been a coincidence, or someone saw what she was doing.

People with emotional issues gain nothing by working with someone who is also emotionally unstable. Judy needed an older man with a soft voice. For all of her strengths, she had a weakness that only a soft-spoken person could reach. A blustery therapist would find Judy withdrawing into her cocoon, not to be seen while they were there.

As I was conversing with my editor, she sent me a note that reminded me of something I had written in some notes a few years back. I had a remarkable father, and the things he taught me were invaluable to me during my life. I miss him every day. This is what I sent back to my editor:

Growing up on a farm, my father taught me how to 'listen' to animals and make them respond the way you want them to respond. I have a dog, Buster, he of the "Go get Dad, Timmy has fallen down the well" fame in the story of my wife. Buster had been a vicious animal when we got him as a rescue pup. It was clear (to me, anyway) that he was afraid. We spoke softly to him and touched him gently, and he has become a very gentle animal, loving and great with kids. As I grew up, I turned that ability with animals into 'listening' to humans.

I wish I could tell you more about the woman I loved, but this is the end of our conversation. I was blessed to have found Judy.

Kenny Rogers did a song long ago that perfectly fits our life together. I can truthfully tell you that "Through the Years," Judy made sure that the sweetest days I found were with her. When everything went wrong, together, we were strong. I can't imagine needing someone as much as I needed her. I learned what life was about by loving her.

I could write another book about our wonderful times together, but this finishes this story, and I need to thank a few people. Just as no man is an island, no writer is complete without their editor. I have to give a huge shout-out to my friend and beta-reader Ginny Pope of Phoenix. I would send her each chapter, and she would edit them and point out my occasional story flaws. I've learned that you can't win an argument with an editor, and I'm glad to have Ginny working with my words as a friend and editor.

I have belonged to a PPV 'writers' club' on Blogit.com since 2002, and virtually everything I write is posted there before it ever hits publication on Amazon. I have to thank so many posters that have supported me there, and I hope not to miss any of them. In no particular order, we have Kabu, RPresta, FormerStudentIntern, C_C_T, TAPS, Sherri_G, and BearCat-Mike. Thank you for your help and your friendship.

Finally, my friends over on X, formerly Twitter! Good grief! I have found hundreds of writing friends–active writers who share the hopes, dreams, and agonies of writing. I can't say enough about my friends at the Fresh Ink Group. Thank you, you, my fellow writers!

If you have enjoyed reading this story, please rate it on Amazon. The best way to show appreciation to an author is to rate their book!

Thank you for reading!

Verwayne Greenhoe
March 2018
Updated June 2024

About Verwayne Greenhoe

Born and raised on a small dairy farm in west-central Michigan, I learned about life and death at an early age. I was lucky enough to have a loving, caring father who taught me about some of the more intricate 'ins and outs' of living every day.

I later became a medic, worked in a prison's psych ward, and spent many years working in Emergency Rooms as an aide and then a nurse. These experiences gave me both the background and insight to write about many things.

I have twenty-eight audiobooks out that you can find on Audible or on Amazon under my listing for stories and books. I try to add a novella of 16,000 to 22,000 words every two or three months and at least two to three 40,000+ word novels every year. 2021 was an exception. I developed a bad case of Parkinson's, and I couldn't get it under control enough to write well enough to do any serious writing. I've got it under control now.

Fresh Ink Group

Independent Multi-media Publisher
Fresh Ink Group / Push Pull Press
Voice of Indie / GeezWriter

Hardcovers
Softcovers
All Ebook Formats
Audiobooks
Podcasts
Worldwide Distribution

Indie Author Services
Book Development, Editing, Proofing
Graphic/Cover Design
Video/Trailer Production
Website Creation
Social Media Marketing
Writing Contests
Writers' Blogs

Authors
Editors
Artists
Experts
Professionals

FreshInkGroup.com
info@FreshInkGroup.com
Twitter: @FreshInkGroup
Facebook.com/FreshInkGroup
LinkedIn: Fresh Ink Group

More by Verwayne Greenhoe

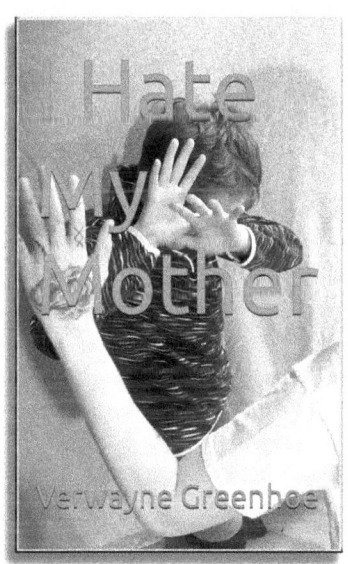

More by Verwayne Greenhoe

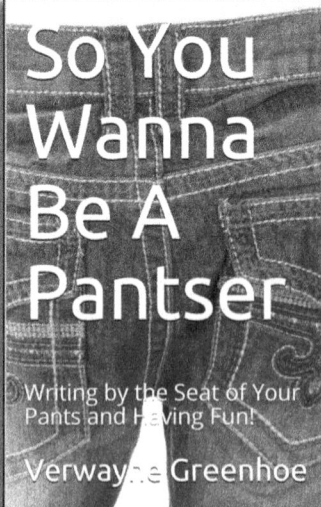

More by Verwayne Greenhoe

More by Verwayne Greenhoe

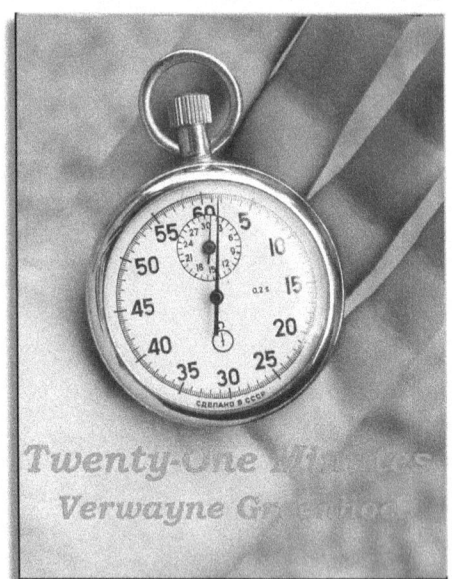

In the Pruitt Igoe slums of St. Louis in the 1960s, a heroin-addict mother breaks her son's dolls and screams, "You are not a girl!" However, no one can convince Stephanie to live as Stephen. Her mother pimps her out to a man who rapes her and takes pictures of her as others rape her. After finding her mother brutally murdered, she is placed in Christian foster care, where they also try to convince her to accept being male. Her mother's lover is sentenced to life in prison for the murder. Famed Televangelist Pastor Ronald Dennison sets up a trust that allows a compassionate old neighbor to adopt her out of foster care. Still, she is violently bullied at school for identifying as female. The trust pays for transition surgery at eighteen, and she begins to live fully as a woman. Frightened by men, she remains a virgin until she falls in love with Jordan, but she runs into the man who abused her and remembers her childhood pledge to kill him. Will her lust for murdering the man who brutalized her as a child cause her to lose the man she loves, or will she come to her senses before it's too late?

Jacketed Hardcover
Softcover
All Ebooks Editions

Milton Keynes UK
Ingram Content Group UK Ltd.
UKHW020229310724
446355UK00010B/84/J